Contents

Children and Books in the Modern World:
Contemporary Perspectives on Literacy

Edited by

Ed Marum

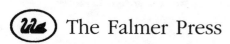 The Falmer Press

(A member of the Taylor & Francis Group)
London • Washington, D.C.

UK   The Falmer Press, 1 Gunpowder Square, London, EC4A 3DE
USA The Falmer Press, Taylor & Francis Inc., 1900 Frost Road, Suite 101, Bristol, PA 19007

First published in 1996

A catalogue record for this book is available from the British Library

Library of Congress Cataloging-in-Publication Data are available on request

ISBN 0 7507 0542 6 cased
ISBN 0 7507 0543 4 paper

Jacket design by Caroline Archer

Typeset in 10/12 pt Garamond by
Graphicraft Typesetters Ltd., Hong Kong

Printed in Great Britain by Biddles Ltd., Guildford and King's Lynn on paper which has a specified pH value on final paper manufacture of not less than 7.5 and is therefore 'acid free'.

Acknowledgments

As ever, the contributors would like to thank colleagues, students and children who have worked with us and helped us define and articulate our views about, and feeling for, the importance of literacy in society.

The editor thanks, in particular, his fellow contributors, who responded positively and enthusiastically at short notice to his invitation to help make this book.

Every attempt has been made to identify sources; these are acknowledged in specific chapters. However, given the final impossibility of knowing all one's sources, one can only acknowledge one's indebtedness:

> The few adults who have really given me something to read have always effaced themselves before the books, and they've always been careful not to ask me what I had understood in these books. To them, of course, I'd talk about what I'd read. To them, be they living or dead, I offer up these pages. (Pennac, D. (1994) *Reads Like A Novel*, London, Quartet Books)

The secret garden was not the only one Dickon worked in. (Burnett, F.H. (1993) *The Secret Garden*, London, Diamond Books)

The world in which our educational system has developed has made immense demands upon it to mould its charges in the image of rationality and the objective standpoint. The tremendous forces unleashed in the productive enterprise of the twentieth century have appeared to require as much from society's operations. This process cannot continue indefinitely. Man as object, as self, has grown through object-reflexive action at the expense of man as subject, as Being. To overcome this disjunction, man as Being must grow. Education must discover a real concern with subject-reflexive action. Subject-reflexive action is the foundation of an intelligence of feeling. (Witkin, R.W. (1981) *The Intelligence of Feeling*, London, Heinemann Educational)

Some people believe that being literate is 'knowing the facts'. My experience reacts against this because I am persuaded that, as human beings, we shall always interpret what we know in the sensitive context of our own human experience, and we shall undoubtedly teach our children to do the same. (Meek, M. (1991) *On Being Literate*, London, The Bodley Head)

Introduction: Literacy Now

Ed Marum

I ended a previous volume on literacy (Marum, 1995) with the following short section entitled 'Towards a Beginning' and, because the present volume is both a continuation and a development of the previous one, I should like to introduce this book with that same section:

> The concept of childhood is not quite dead. If the inevitable pressures upon young people will continue to accelerate their premature desires for the imagined worlds of adolescence and maturity, it will be all the more important that the formal education they receive should seek to directly address the 'specific conditions of their lives' from nursery to secondary schooling. If the other face of innocence is enquiry, educators must acknowledge and act upon the very real enthusiasm for learning that young people regularly, and often despite the odds, display. They must, above all, radically change their practice to retain and stimulate that enthusiasm through the years of formal schooling.

We need, in the first instance, a new generation of teachers who are 'multiliterate' in the sense I have identified, and who will be able and willing to inform and guide children and adolescents in the new kind of partnership learning requires. Our approach to the literacies of the future will both condition and reflect the kind of society we wish to be. We will need to acknowledge the truth about our condition, rather than to erect still more false windmills to tilt at. English teachers, above all others, must be able to stand in unity with Pennac (1994):

> Man builds houses because he is alive, but he writes books because he knows he's mortal. He lives in groups because he is gregarious, but he reads because he knows he's alone. His reading keeps him company, but without replacing any other; rather no other company can take its place. Reading offers him no definitive explanation of his fate, but weaves a tight network of correspondences between life and him. These correspondences, tiny and secretive, speak of the paradoxical good fortune of being alive, even while they're illuminating the tragic absurdity of life. The result is that our reasons for reading are quite as strange as are our reasons for living. And no one is charged to have us render an account of that intimate strangeness. (pp. 177–8)

The first step that English teachers must now take is to acknowledge the situation they are in before they go on to change it. The first part of that process is not yet complete. The contributors to this book hope that they have helped to identify ways forward in the process of facing some of the problems that need to be addressed. This is not a new situation; nor is it a hopeless one:

> Problem-posing education is revolutionary futurity. Hence it is pro-
> phetic (and, as such, hopeful), and so corresponds to the historical
> nature of man (sic). Thus, it affirms men as beings who transcend
> themselves, who move forward and look ahead, for whom immobil-
> ity represents a fatal threat, for whom looking at the past must only
> be a means of understanding more clearly what and who they are so
> that they can more wisely build the future . . . The point of departure
> of the movement lies in men themselves. But since men do not exist
> apart from the world, apart from reality, the movement must begin in
> the 'here and now', which constitutes the situation within which they
> are submerged, from which they emerge, and in which they intervene.
> Only by starting from this situation — which determines their percep-
> tion of it — can they begin to move. To do this authentically they
> must perceive their state not as fated and unalterable, but merely as
> limiting — and therefore challenging. (Freire, 1972, p. 57)

The most important current challenge for English teachers is clear. A great deal depends on their response. Future literacies, as part of our understanding of 'cultures', are even now in the process of redefinition outside the classroom. Like the concept of 'literacy', that of 'culture' will 'come to have different meanings while it is still in use' (Scafe, 1989, p. 22).

Because literacies will become increasingly important in our understanding of future 'cultures', and because the latter will in a very real sense shape our understanding of our collective world future, we might do worse than to make a beginning by reminding ourselves of the words of Raymond Williams (1958):

> The word culture cannot automatically be pressed into service as any
> kind of social or personal directive. Its emergence in its modern mean-
> ings marks the effort at total qualitative assessment, but what it indic-
> ates is a process not a conclusion. (p. 285)

All the above is not to say that literacy is the sole province of teachers (a point the contributors to this volume go on to develop in some detail). However, the role of the teacher remains central to our understanding of what literacy is. In a schooling society the teacher will continue to be an important influence upon our definition of literacy and a central agent in its mediation in learning. It is important, therefore, that the teacher has both a view of what literacy means and a strategy for its teaching. I believe this book shows that this is not the simple matter which it at first seems.

We need to begin the process of change by recognizing that old strategies based only on the ability to make meaning from print will no longer do. Since we are aware that what we call literacy is not a static phenomenon and that it will continue to change in the future, we need in consequence some new teachers as well as some new teaching. And this is far from belittling those thousands of teachers who daily give of their best, despite difficult conditions, in classrooms around the world: I, with many others, have cause to be grateful to them. But as society continues to change new literacies continue to emerge. This in turn demands a new type of training for tomorrow's teachers, and a new awareness that unless such training is provided and a fresh look is taken at our views on literacy, tomorrow's pupils and students will be sold short. This is what I meant when I said in the section above that in future we will need 'multiliterate' teachers. What I mean by this term, and the type of teachers and teaching that will be required, are among the issues addressed in this book. However, before the contributors go on to develop specific arguments from the basis of their individual perspectives on literacy, I should like to provide a brief explanation of the book's contents.

It has been my deliberate intention to include chapters written from American, British and European perspectives. In an obvious sense the distinction between Britain and Europe is, of course, artificial, but it is made (in the opening section only) because of the current debate on literacy which has been generated by the introduction and development of National Curriculum proposals for England and Wales during the 1990s, and which continues to be of central educational importance to all involved with literacy issues in Britain (for a fuller discussion of these issues see Marum, 1995). In all other respects, the views on literacy issues in Britain contained here may, I believe, be usefully set alongside the other American and European views on the subject provided by colleague-contributors to this book. In part, therefore, the book hopes to provide a comparative and contemporary perspective on literacy. Hence its title.

However, another intention behind the book is to allow readers the opportunity to move beyond a comparative perspective to consider the wider social and cultural issues of literacy in society. In this sense, I believe the essays taken together create a network of issues for further discussion, research and development. Again, the book is unusual in that it brings together chapters which are at times reflective, in the historical as well as the personal sense; at times they are radical in their suggestions on and implications for the future teaching of literacies; and on other occasions they report specific research findings in some detail. Collectively, the book attempts to bring these chapters together so that literacy development is seen in the multiple contexts of its history, of its research, and of the practical issues relating to books, film and other media — all of which focus our attention on what we mean by literacy now.

Despite the necessary and valuable differences in perspective which are reflected in the chapters, there is also much that they share in common — a concern for people's and societies' future needs, a real engagement with teaching and learning, an examination of the suitability of contemporary curricula and of teachers' practices in a variety of situations. What I believe emerges are discernible patterns and themes which are truly international and which affect the teaching and learning of literacies wherever they take place. What also clearly emerges from the chapters which follow is a surprising consensus of approach across countries and cultures — the national, political and social implications surrounding attitudes to literacy are seen to be of immense importance, whatever the detailed difference in the curricula of individual countries as they are described. That is, the process of schooling provides one, perhaps traditional, perspective on literacy; society at large provides others. Those in education can no longer afford to ignore the huge importance of the latter. Beyond this obvious fact, I believe the book seeks to ask the important question of the future of literacy: what will it mean for us, as teachers and learners, as it changes our world?

References

FREIRE, P. (1972) *Pedagogy of the Oppressed*, Harmondsworth, Penguin Books.

MARUM, E. (1995) *Towards 2000: The Future of Childhood, Literacy and Schooling*, London, Falmer Press.

PENNAC, D. (1994) *Reads Like A Novel* (trans. Gunn, D.), London, Quartet Books.

SCAFE, S. (1989) *Teaching Black Literature*, London, Virago Press.

WILLIAMS, R. (1958) *Culture and Society*, Harmondsworth, Penguin Books.

Section 1

National Perspectives on Literacy Policy

1 Literacy: Its Roller-coaster Ride through US Education

John S. Simmons

When one embarks on an undertaking as vast and complex as tracing the trail of literacy in US education, one must set a few parameters. For the first, I choose a somewhat cowardly one: a review of dictionary pronouncements. One old standby, the *American Collegiate Dictionary* (1970) (published by Random House) offers the following:

> literacy — the state of being literate; possession of an education; literate — ability to read and write; having an education; educated; one who can read and write

For a more recent definition, what better place to turn than the offerings of that concerned, venerable colonist Noah Webster? In the *Ninth New Collegiate Dictionary* (1987) (published by Miriam-Webster) Webster's descendants provide this:

> literacy — the quality or state of being literate; literate — educated, cultured; able to read and write; versed in literature or creative writing . . . an educated person

While some may regard the above as sprawling and unhelpful, it is my feeling that, for my argument, some useful seeds are sewn in the objective multiple definitions.

Second caveat: the delimitation of time. Following the path chosen by so many chroniclers of political, social, cultural and educational conditions, I shall begin my review/critique of the care and feeding of literacy as a major educational outcome with the end of World War II, a decision which represents more than a merely quantitatively convenient one or even a culmination of the '50-year anniversary' celebration so recently observed by most of the victorious Western democracies. In fact, the half century which began with the August 1945 surrender of the Japanese empire in Tokyo Bay set in motion a whole series of dramatic, often rapid, and broadly affective movements in US education from very early childhood all the way to the doctoral levels. Speaking as one who was about to enter public high school when the big bombs

7

fell on Hiroshima and Nagasaki, I can personally attest to the breadth and significance of those changes.

Final disclaimer: the nature and limitations of *this* chronicler. My abbreviated vitae discloses that I have, since 1957, been a teacher, teacher educator, and researcher in the English language arts, grades 6 through 12 (ages 11 through 18). I have never taught children below age 11, nor do I know much about their diverse linguistic needs/capacities beyond my fatherhood involvements of yore. Thus, if I offer what may seem to some a somewhat narrow perspective, they are right on target. As Pope states in *An Essay on Man*, 'the part cannot comprehend the whole'. With the above cop-outs thus recited, let the chronicle begin.

The Decline of Progressivism: 1945–1955

As the war drew to a close, so did the considerable influence of those educators called progressivists (often derisively), which was clearly waning. The grim realities of the Depression and the frenetic demands on the populace from the Pearl Harbor catastrophe had given rise in US education to a survivalist curricular mentality. The pre-Depression classical curriculum — dominated by the study of ancient languages, the 'great books' of literary (European) authors, history of western civilization — was replaced by a more contemporary, pragmatic, largely pre-vocational model. The pragmatism of William James, the *weltanschauung* of John Dewey, the spirit of Rousseau, and the pangs of hunger — all contributed to a radical change in programs of study coast to coast. They reflected the goal of education as preparation for the world of work and enlightened citizenship. In this emerging curriculum, literacy had to do with the language of the workplace and of local/state/national political imperatives rather than the translation of Cicero, the parsing of compound sentences, or the appreciative essay on *Ivanhoe.*

Some educational catchphrases and buzz words became labels for the shift noted above. Terms such as 'core curriculum', 'common learnings' and 'citizenship training' were reflective of the Jamesian pragmatism and the relevance of tenets in Dewey's *Experience and Education* (1933). In the study of English, the 1935 publication by the National Council of Teachers of English[1] of Wilbur Hatfield's *An Experience Curriculum in English* proposed a new look in that area of study wherein the term 'language arts' was evolved to define the need for and ways of teaching the four major communication skills: reading, writing, speaking and listening. The study of celebrated literary texts, as well as the use of classical models of rhetoric in teaching writing, became largely irrelevant. Also the long-standing but largely secretive distrust of Latinate grammar and rigidly correct usage as the way to 'do language' began to come out of the closet, albeit furtively. Still the brand of literacy propounded by these change agents was often sterile or formulaic. The case for English instruction as reflective of humanistic themes found a strong and unequivocal voice in Dora V. Smith's *Communication: The Miracle of Shared Living* (1941), in Angela Broening's *Conducting Experiences in English* (1939), and in a then-overlooked text on the nature, place and value of literature, Louise Rosenblatt's *Literature as Exploration* (1938). It took forty years of dormancy for the Rosenblatt book to have its legitimate impact on the teaching-of-English gentry. Characteristic of the times, however, it concentrated on the transaction between text and the individual reader as a means of assisting in the aesthetic, social, emotional and intellectual development of the latter.

Humanistic dimensions notwithstanding, it was the pragmatic *Education for All American Youth*[2] approach to literacy attainment which greeted the GIs upon their triumphant return to the States from Europe and the Far East. Wasn't it the chemistry profs, however, who taught us that for every action, there is a reaction? The apologists for the sanctity of the Great Books approach to literacy naturally found progressivist thinking intolerable and, in the mid 1940s, began to strike back at the language arts/communication skills brands of literacy teaching in both public debate and printed attacks on this pragmatic dilution of the quality of literacy instruction. It is striking to note the similarities between the pragmatist/academic conflict of this era and the functional literacy/cultural literacy struggle of the 1970s and 1980s, which will be described later. Maybe there is something to the cyclical theory of culture after all. In the 1940s and 50s, however, it became abundantly clear that many traditional academics were disturbed at the inherent threat this approach seemingly represented to traditional academic disciplines. Thus, the period from 1944 to the late 1950s spurred a 'great debate' in American education during which many teachers trained in liberal arts and science disciplines found it increasingly difficult to teach within this 'life adjustment' approach.

The 'great debate' accelerated between 1949 and the mid-1950s when books like Mortimer Smith's *And Madly Teach* (1949) complained that progressive education (as represented by the life adjustment movement) had become 'the official philosophy of American public education' and characterized teachers, administrators and schools of education as having a 'truly amazingly uniformative opinion regarding the aims, the content and the methods of education' (p. 37). Books and rhetoric such as this prompted the formation of organizations like the Council for Basic Education which entered the fray in 1956 and championed educational conservatism.

The membership of the Council for Basic Education was made up largely of professors teaching at various universities, editors, journalists and several self-appointed critics who feared the takeover of all public education by Deweyan apostles and, as they saw it, the inevitable 'watering down' of the curriculum:

> The Council for Basic Education was established in the belief that the purpose of education is the harmonious development of the mind, the will, and the conscience of each individual so that he may use to the fullest his intrinsic powers and shoulder the responsibilities of

citizenship . . . It insists that only by the maintenance of high academic standards can the ideal of democratic education be realized. (Lynch and Evans, 1963, p. 24)

In two monographs which led to the founding of the Council for Basic Education, *And Madly Teach* (Smith, 1949) and *Educational Wastelands* (Bestor, 1953), the National Council of Teachers of English (NCTE) was upbraided as one of the chief proponents of creeping mediocrity in public school curriculum development. As US society settled down to a period of unparalleled prosperity, tempered by the growing uneasiness of Cold War confrontations on several continents, the need for reassessing the rubrics of literacy as provided to the children and adolescents entering public schools became more evident. The growth in affluence, the evolution of suburbia, the availability of the GI Bill of Rights to young men and women from all walks of life, all led to the dramatic increase in the demand for, and creation of, higher education opportunities from coast to coast and border to border.

As the possibilities of receiving college degrees became a reality, and funds for tuition, etc., became available, one of the emerging *curricular* needs was that of literacy enhancement, i.e., training, which would assist this 'breed' of college student with the abilities to read dense subject-matter textbooks and to meet the formidable writing demands of Freshman Composition and term papers in academic courses. All of these new priorities sounded the death knell for progressivism in general and the *Experience Curriculum* brand of literacy teaching in particular.

Before moving on to a very different definition of literacy, US variety, another sociopolitical event demands some attention — that of Civil Rights. After the Japanese surrender in 1945, the GIs did come marching home. Many of these defenders of freedom were members of minority groups — African American, Hispanic, Native American, Asiatic — to name the four most prominent ones. Slavery, the Jim Crow laws, and Southern white terrorism had placed the Civil Rights spotlight squarely on the Negro citizens (as they were called in those days). Their claim to a piece of the post-war action was not wildly acclaimed, especially in the Deep South where a cadre of senior US Congressmen held chairs on vital legislative committees. Still, in 1946, Jackie Robinson broke into major league baseball, the GI Bill and loan programs were provided to *all* veterans, and the 1948 Democratic Party included a strong Civil Rights plank — causing a splinter group from Dixie to leave and nominate their own presidential candidate, and, in fact, initiate the slow but inexorable movement of white Southerners to the Grand Old (Republican) Party.

It was probably from this point that one of the great schisms began to develop in American curricula. The question, 'Should literacy instruction be directed primarily to the needs of these disadvantaged youth whose racial origins caused them to be linguistically deficient or should it serve increasingly larger numbers of young white people who were now becoming candidates for baccalaureate degrees which in turn guaranteed them several rungs up the socioeconomic ladder?' That question is an undeniable adjunct to the battle over racial equality in the USA, a conflict which, if anything, has intensified in this century, as the divided opinion of the OJ Simpson trial, raging as this is written, will verify.

Literacy in the Pursuit of Scholarly Expression

As the 50s ran their course, mostly under the paternal gaze of Dwight Eisenhower, it became increasingly evident that Deweyan progressivism was done for and that the elitist attitudes of the CBE apostles were increasing their influence on literacy instructional objectives. The 1954 Supreme Court decision outlawing school segregation everywhere, and the Martin Luther King-led movement to unseat Jim Crow laws in the states of the Old Confederacy (1955) were not really considered in the move to make literacy a more academically respectable pursuit. In the year 1957, certain events transpired to accelerate that thrust.

On 4 October of that year, six days after President Eisenhower had ordered Little Rock Central High School (Arkansas) forcibly integrated, the Soviet Union propelled into orbit an unmanned space object which became known the world over as Sputnik. This aerospace triumph sent shockwaves through the US education establishment. Soon a number of events transpired to move the literacy issue toward academic control:

(i) The US Congress established the National Defense Education Act providing federal support for all high school academic areas including English (eventually).

(ii) The NCTE presented the result of a study titled *The National Interest and the Teaching of English* which presented a dismal picture of English instruction nationally and urged federal assistance.

(iii) The prestigious College Entrance Examination Board formed a Commission on English which organized a series of summer institutes for English teachers. It also began to develop a number of kinescopes (the forerunner to videotape) which featured scholarly lectures by university professors on how to present 'teachable' literary classics in high school.

(iv) The US Office of Education, through its Cooperative Research division, inaugurated funding for a number of Curriculum Study Centers in English, all at major research universities, all dedicated to the production of instructional units which would reflect a more vigorous approach to the teaching of the discipline.

(v) The Basic Issues Conference, held in the wake of the national reaction to the Sputnik launch, deserves particular attention; it articulated the direction literacy instructional theory would follow for the next decade, with the encouragement of the US Office of Education. JN Hook, Executive Secretary of that organization, had arranged a conference on the pressing needs of the English curriculum with three other US professional organizations: the Modern Language Association, the American Studies Association and the College English Association. Three such (three-day) meetings were held, all at Carnegie Mellon Institute in Pittsburgh, Pennsylvania. They were called the Basic Issues Conferences, and the first took place in late January 1958.

Of the twenty-eight invited participants to this conference, twenty-three were college or university professors of English. One professor of elementary education, one professor of English education, one superintendent of public schools (suburban Chicago), and two high school English teachers completed the roster. The heavy preponderance of college English teachers is significant; the growing demand for rigor in the English curriculum was clearly evident in the nature of this selection process.

The strong academic tone of the conference became clear in the main document promulgated by its participants. They presented a list (and amplification) of thirty-five basic issues having to do with the proper teaching of the discipline. Of these, the first two are the most significant and general. They are:

(i) *What is 'English'?* We agree generally that English composition, language and literature are within our province, but we are uncertain whether our boundaries should include world literature in translation, public speaking, journalism, listening, remedial reading and general academic orientation. Some of these activities admittedly promote the social development of the individual. But does excessive emphasis on them result in the neglect of that great body of literature which can point the individual's development in more significant directions? Has the fundamental liberal discipline of English been replaced, at some levels of schooling, by *ad hoc* training in how to write a letter, how to give a radio speech, manners, dating, telephoning, vocational guidance?

(ii) *Can basic programs in English be devised that are sequential and cumulative from the kindergarten through the graduate school?* Can agreement be reached upon a body of knowledge and set of skills as standard at certain points in the curriculum, making due allowances for flexibility of planning, individual differences, and patterns of growth? This issue seems crucial to this entire document and to any serious approach to the problem. Unless we can find an answer to it, we must resign ourselves to an unhappy future in which the present curricular disorder persists and the whole liberal discipline of English continues to disintegrate and lose its character. Within this basic issue are such sub-issues as: What assumptions, if any, should the teacher *at any level* be able to make about the training his students have received at lower levels? How much responsibility does the teacher at any level have to prepare his students for the next higher level? Who sees to it that the work in the elementary school is related to that in secondary school, the work on the secondary school level to that of the elementary school and of college, the work in college to that of the high school and the graduate school?[3]

With these two questions and their answers, a trend was established in the theorizing about the teaching of English which would last for the better part of ten years (and would, concurrently, ignore the pressing curricular needs of newly integrated schools). The answer to Basic Issue (i) set in motion a curriculum concept called the 'tri-component', or 'tripod' model; i.e., English is language, literature, and composition — and nothing else. Words such as skills, language arts, and communication virtually ceased to exist as the tri-component model was refined and expanded in the professional literature of the years immediately following. This model was also to become the lightning rod for federal support which would soon shower down on the English teaching establishment in unprecedented amounts.

The main text to emerge from the conference was *Issues, Problems and Approaches in the Teaching of English* by Professor George Winchester Stone, Jr. (published by Holt, Rinehart & Winston). Dr. Stone was the Executive Secretary of the Modern Language Association, the bastion of academic English study for college and university teachers. The bulk of this text is a series of highly esoteric articles on linguistic and literary study, none of which were outcomes of the Basic Issues conference. Stone's opening section does, however, summarize the thinking of the conference and provides a clear illustration of the academic emphases to be placed on English curricular theory in the years to come.

Thus literacy, during the ten-fifteen years to follow, would take on a distinctly academic definition. Reading would have little to do with basal materials, diagnostic inventories, or word recognition strategies. Nor would it refer to materials from the vocational, mass media, or citizenship elements of Americans' lives. In the public school English curriculum, it would be embodied in the examination of works of high quality; i.e., it would be closely related to belles lettres. Writing would be most closely tied to those intellectual exercises which demanded that students offer coherent papers in which they demonstrated their abilities to analyze and interpret meaning in these texts as well as their appreciation for the literary majesty within them. There has probably been no time in this half-century when perceptions of what literacy meant were more separate; the theorists clinging to their lofty tri-component models, the classroom teachers attempting to deal with the curricular impact of school integration, suburban flight/urban blight, increasingly multicultural student populations, and other reflections of the US in a state of cultural flux.

A clear indication of the thinking of this era could be found in the 'Project English' Curriculum Study Centers. From 1959–70, the United States Office of Education (USOE) funded some twenty-two of these centers, all on university campuses, all run by university professors, few with any input from classroom teachers. While generalizations are always suspect, a few can legitimately be made about the Curriculum Study Centers as a whole.

(i)   Most followed the sequential-cumulative thinking of the Brunerian theorists.

(ii)   Most emphasized a tri-component model of English instruction.

(iii) Most developed materials for students of at least average and usually above-average ability. Only one center, the one at Carnegie-Mellon Institute (Pittsburgh, Pennsylvania) specified that particular target audience.

(iv)   Most sought only to produce materials. Only the center at Florida State University proposed the goal of testing approaches, and only that center did so in a systematic manner.

(v)   Most developed materials for students of average or above-average socioeconomic backgrounds. Only Hunter College produced materials specifically for deprived youth.

(vi)   Most established their target audiences as students in secondary schools (grades 7 through 12; ages 12–17). Only the University of Georgia chose a population of purely elementary school age (6–11) for which to produce instructional materials.

(vii) Most produced materials were 'teacher proof'; i.e., few classroom teachers were over-involved in either the writing or the evaluation of the materials.

(viii) Most paid little attention to production of materials to enhance oral language or basic silent reading skills.

(ix)   Most did little with the treatment or use of adolescent (young adult) fiction in the development of their overall literature scheme.

(x)   Most featured instruction in transformational-generative grammar as their main element in linguistic instruction.

(xi)   Most relied on the new rhetoric, as espoused by Fogarty *et al.* in their production of composition instruction.

Probably the most significant document to appear in print during that year, however, was the text, *Freedom and Discipline in English* by the Commission on English (CEEB; chaired by Harold Martin). This report had been a long time in preparation. The commission had been gathering data for it since the CEEB had established it in 1959. In effect, it pulls together the academically oriented, tri-component, English-for-the-more-fortunate thinking of the decade, which essentially began with the launching of Sputnik in 1957. Its authors came from the ranks of prestigious high schools, preparatory schools, and colleges in the Northeast, with a couple of add-ons from other regions. The tone of this document is strictly elitist. In the very first paragraph of its opening chapter, this tone is evident:

> *What is English?* The Commission on English was appointed by the College Entrance Examination Board in September 1959. Broadly stated, the Commission's purpose was to improve the teaching of English in America's schools and colleges. It sought to encourage and facilitate a gradual nationwide improvement in curriculum, teacher training, and the methods of classroom instruction. Its stated goal was to propose standards of achievement for college preparatory students and to suggest ways of meeting them. The Commission's concern with college preparatory courses in secondary schools may seem to have been narrow, but experience with students in the College Board Advanced Placement Program continues to reveal that better teaching of able students affects the whole schools. The Commission's efforts, then, though aimed at one group, are intended to influence all tracks and all levels. ('The quality of instruction in English' in *Freedom and Discipline in English*, 1965, p. 1)

Soon after that proclamation, the authors state their definition of English:

> What is the school and college subject called *English?* This question the Commission took as its starting point. The report that follows provides an answer arrived at largely by discussion among its members and with hundreds of teachers. The answer rests on the unstartling assumption that language, primarily the English language, constitutes the core of the subject; and on the further and equally unstartling assumption that the study and use of the English language is the proper content of the English curriculum. (*ibid.*, p. 2)

And the attitude held by the authors toward new directions and innovation comes through loud and clear in *this* passage:

> For English the situation is quite different. 'English must be kept up,' wrote Keats; but keeping it up is not primarily a matter of keeping it up to date. To a large degree, the study of English or of any of those subjects loosely classified as the humanities is not a matter of making new, but of constant renewal, constant rediscovery, constant restoration. The sciences and mathematics lose their relevance if they fail to keep close to the working front of their disciplines. The humanities most often suffer from having their essence diluted or obscured by what appears to be new. This is not to say that current knowledge has no meaning for the humanities, but only to insist that the accumulation of the past is for them far richer than for the sciences. Yet,

precisely because the humanities, the study of one's native language and literature among them, are so thoroughly implicated in everyday human activity, they are highly susceptible to immediate and ephemeral influences. The fashion of a time often so overlays them, particularly in their popular forms, that their real nature is all but lost sight of. The English curriculum in the average secondary school today is an unhappy combination of old matter unrenewed and new matter that rarely rises above the level of passing concerns. *Macbeth* vies with the writing of thank-you notes for time in the curriculum, and lessons on telephoning with instruction in the process of argument. (*ibid.*, p. 3)

The chapters which follow the introductory one of *Freedom and Discipline in English* are labelled 'language', 'literature', and 'composition'. As might be assumed from their titles, they provide an elaborate rationale for and description of the tri-component approach as being the way to go for the children and adolescents who were enrolled in the public schools' English classes of that day. Language study focused on the assimilation of modern grammatical systems and the mandatory assumption of correct usage. 'Works of high quality' is the dominant recommendation in their literature chapter. Their chapter on composition represents a plea to teachers to follow the classical models and to prescribe rather rigidly both the content and the form of their students' writing.

It is also worth noting some things which the authors of *Freedom and Discipline in English* either overlook or find inappropriate. The needs of basic or disadvantaged students are never mentioned. Oral activities are seldom described. Suggestions for instruction in reading or basic composition techniques are nowhere to be found. Of adolescent literature, the authors have the following opinion:

Claims are frequently advanced for the use of so-called 'junior books', a 'literature of adolescence', on the ground that they ease the young reader into a frame of mind in which he will tackle something stronger, harder, and more adult. The Commission has serious doubts that it does anything of the sort. For classes in remedial reading a resort to such books may be necessary, but to make them a considerable part of the curriculum for most students is to subvert the purposes for which literature is included in the first place. (*ibid.*, p. 49)

Thus the direction taken by theorists to move the curriculum toward 'excellence' in the narrowly academic sense of the word found its accumulated voice in this document. The apostles of that brand of thinking had clearly forgotten the event of Little Rock Central High School and seemed scarcely concerned about its ramifications. The events which took place in the 'real word' of American public life in 1965, however, suggested the need for a radically different model.

One of the results of the new-found (and short-lived) federal subsidies for English teachers was the decision on the part of some professional leaders to organize a first-ever meeting of British, US, and Canadian English teaching spokespersons. The time seemed right, and the funds were available.

Dartmouth College is a small, aristocratic (by US standards) liberal arts college set in the green, rolling hills near Hanover, New Hampshire. It is the smallest of that cluster of venerated institutions called the Ivy League, and, geographically, it is the most remote from urban civilization. Situated about 125 miles northwest of Boston, it is hard to get to and harder (so say the Dartmouth students) to escape. There are no cities of any appreciable size either in New Hampshire or in neighboring Vermont. In winter, the intense cold and heavy, frequent snows make the place even more inaccessible. In 1966, it was still a college exclusively for men.

So it was to this place in late August of 1966, that forty-nine English scholars/educators travelled to participate in the Anglo-American Seminar on the Teaching of English. Sponsored by NCTE and MLA, from the US jointly with the newer (1952) NATE of the UK, it was funded primarily by the Carnegie Corporation of New York. Of the forty-nine full-time participants, twenty-eight were from the United States, twenty from the UK, and one from Canada. Interestingly thirteen of the twenty British participants had within their stated titles the word 'education', and several listed experience work in what are called in the US *public schools*. The Canadian, Merron Chorny, presented similar credentials. The Americans, on the other hand, were dominated by university scholars. Of the twenty-four participating, fifteen were from the 'scholarly' ranks, while only seven were affiliated with colleges of education of the public schools on a full-time basis. The two NCTE officials present could not legitimately be listed in either category. In the often heated dialogue, which has since become the emblem of the Dartmouth Conference, this difference must surely have been a factor.

Despite the fact that the meeting was held on American soil, supported largely by American dollars, and attended by a solid majority of American educators (in addition to the forty-eight participants, there are listed twenty-two consultants, fourteen of whom were from the US), the meeting had a distinctly British flavor from the outset. The flavor was symbolized by its location. NATE meetings are usually held on college campuses when no students are around. The participants live in dormitories rather than posh downtown hotels and eat (and drink) a simple fare. No publishers provide elaborate exhibits or lavish cocktail parties. The numbers are relatively small when compared to the annual NCTE/MLA extravaganzas, and the tone is serious throughout.

Probably more indicative of the predominantly British atmosphere was the nature of the meetings. Plenary sessions (that's code for long-winded, carefully prepared papers redolent of esoterica) were few in number. Most of the time was spent in working parties, small study groups, and seminars wherein all in attendance had a voice. As Albert Marckwardt notes in his Foreword to John Dixon's first edition of *Growth Through English*,

Beyond this, anyone was free to nominate himself to conduct a meeting, open or closed, on any topic germane to the overall purpose of the Seminar, and the surprising thing was that people came in respectable numbers to listen. Participants were equally free to express their views in writing, and it is no exaggeration to say that the conference secretaries were worked to a point of exhaustion. In order that discussion might get down to earth instead of remaining suspended on an abstract plane, the entire conference examined and evaluated samples of student writing and also split up into groups for the analysis of poems, though perhaps not as often as it should have. (Foreword, p. viii)

And the voices were often strident. From all reports rendered since, the arguments rose to fever pitch every day and in virtually every gathering. During the entire four-week session, points of contrast between the two national approaches came frequently and joltingly to the fore. The reasons for the ongoing adversarial dialogue are really quite obvious. The difference in professional roles of the two groups has already been noted. The curricular philosophies were also in sharp contrast. The Americans brought to the seminar an academically oriented view of English for young people. Given the prestige-university backgrounds and utter lack of either understanding of or sympathy for the nature of elementary or secondary schools, their perspective should come as no surprise. To bolster this position, they came armed to the teeth with their tri-component, Brunerian project English materials, *none* of which had been truly tested by August 1966. The British countered with a language experience, growth, and development, student-centered approach which held tight, academic prescription in total disregard. It was probably the first time in their tenure as curricular pundits that these mastodons of US English scholarship and teaching had been seriously questioned about the rationale and nature of the project English brainchildren. Surely no lowly classroom teachers had had the temerity, or indeed been given the opportunity to do so. Their greatest shock must have come in the awareness that their British (and Canadian) counterparts would so vigorously contest their fundamental assumptions of what English was or should do. Whereas at the Basic Issues Conference of 1958 they solemnly agreed throughout as to the validity of the academic model for all students, now they were facing disagreement which was cogent, articulate, and unrelenting.

Literacy in a Skinnerian Maze

The impact of the Dartmouth seminar on English educationists in the USA was considerable. In the years following the meeting, student-centered approaches, writing as a broad-based means of expression, heightened interest in oral and dramatic classroom activities, and diminished faith in 'teacher proof' materials all rose in stature. Thus the belief that literacy had to do primarily with understanding and expressing aspects of the *human* situation largely replaced the student-as-scholar one in the minds — and writings — of those educators.

The real world shift in perspectives on literacy, however, came from a different and implacable source: the American body politic. Increasingly disenchanted with the 'liberal' initiatives of the Kennedy-Johnson administrations, the voters struck back. In the off-year elections of 1966, they punished a number of moderate-to-liberal governors and senators. Conservative legislators were sent to both houses of Congress, a novice politician named Ronald Reagan took the California governorship in a landslide, and an equally inexperienced individual named Claude Kirk won the governor's race in Florida, becoming the first Republican elected to statewide office in the Deep South since the Reconstruction era. Then, in 1968, Richard Nixon won a narrow victory over Hubert Humphrey and segregationist George Wallace to end the Great Society direction of the past decade.

One of the marked changes in the Nixon age was the manner in which literacy was defined. At the USOE, the Ivy League economists, literary scholars, and historians cleaned out their offices and were largely replaced by behavioral psychologists from such 'mainstream' US campuses as Ohio State, Nebraska and the University of Texas. Their concern was not with preserving elitist notions but to goad schools into getting more for the education dollar. The term which emanated from Washington, DC in those days was accountability, which has been used as a switch with which to thrash unfocused educators for the last quarter century. Literacy was conveyed through the advancement of basic skills: in reading, writing, and computation. Reading instruction, under the behavioralist commitment to Individually Prescribed Instruction (IPI), was suddenly systems-driven. Behavioral objectives, spelled out in observable, quantified criteria, set in motion all reading/writing instruction. In many states, curricular theorists alluded to students as products. Hand-in-hand with this movement was the growth of an objective testing mania which has persisted through the years and is riding high as we prepare to enter the twenty-first century.

In the previous paragraph, the direction of 'the states' in the educational shift was noted. In fact, new federal legislation promulgated the Education Professional Development Act (EPDA) to replace the NDEA as the major funding mechanism for education. One of the main directives of the EPDA leaders was to give to the fifty states more autonomy in using the reduced funds now being provided. The states responded by establishing the Education Commission of the States, a group populated by the governors and education commissioners from each sovereign body. One of the first acts was to create a testing agency titled the National Assessment of Educational Progress which, in 1970, produced a nine-part instrument, seven of which dealt directly or indirectly with literacy. Needless to say, the mechanism was 100 per cent 'fill in the dots completely'; in only one test were the students asked to write so much as a word.

As the basic skills, competency-based, IPI movement enveloped the land, a new literacy label emerged: functional literacy. This umbrella term included the teaching of reading (mostly non-literary), traditional Latinate grammar (the cornerstone of writing 'correctly'), study skills, writing about the contemporary environment (especially the world of *work*), and a few 'useful' oral activities, such as the staged job interview. Literature, imaginative writing, and creative oral activity became back-burner enterprises.

Part of the functional literacy endeavor included a new emphasis on the writing process as a desirable classroom enterprise. Support for this aspect of literary development came from an unlikely source: the National Writing Project. Begun as the Bay Area Writing Project in Berkeley, California in 1973, this innovative program put teachers in charge of the learning process instead of the prof. Teachers, both in summer institutes and periodic year-round meetings, write together, respond to peers' writing, present original instructional schemes, and in general show what they know about the nature, process and evaluation of writing. From humble (financially speaking) beginnings, it soon became the National Writing Project, received support from the National Endowment for the Humanities (now threatened by the axe wielding Newt Gingrich), and is today financed primarily by the contributions of local school districts. The teachers from these districts then assume the responsibility for educating teachers in *their* schools. Thus the project has fanned out across the country and touched the lives of well over 100,000 teachers, kindergarten through college. Whatever its future, the NWP has had a leadership role in promoting the writing process in lieu of labelling parts of speech and diagramming sentences.

While the writing projects of the seventies were influencing small groups of US teachers here and there, the vast majority of classroom purveyors of literacy across the grade levels were being led ('dragged' may be a more appropriate verb) to 'do' literacy in a decidedly Skinnerian behavioralist mode. The EPDA, as noted previously, had placed educational support *and philosophical slant* in the hands of the state educationist bureaucrats. Soon, state after state legislature was enacting accountability mandates, laws with two prominent goals: (i) to achieve minimum competencies in the basic skills (reading, writing, computation); and (ii) to attach testing components to the instructional package.

In 1972 such an act was passed in the State of Florida. After five years of bickering, civil rights challenges, and often bewildering amendments, a set of statewide competency tests was administered to children at grades 3, 5, 8 and 11 (ages 8, 10, 13 and 16). The eleventh grade test was supplemented by a functional literacy instrument. What made the latter a daunting one to the state's high school administrators and teachers was that a minimum passing score became a credential for graduation. Civil Rights leaders from Florida's large African-American and Hispanic minority populations quickly filed suit in federal court claiming primarily that the test was 'culturally biased'. A federal district court in Florida ruled, in 1982, that the test scores could in fact be used as graduation criteria, and the decision was upheld in the 11th US Circuit Court of Appeals in 1983. The minority litigants threw in the towel at that point, and an arbitrary passing score remained a prerequisite to high school graduation until 1991, when the original 1977 testing apparatus was thrown out, and the creation of a new one became the focus of the evaluation/assessment experts in the Florida Department of Education.

The Florida testing apparatus is important because it set in motion the national testing mania which had been festering since the 1968 accountability urge commenced. By 1980 all fifty states were administering tests, minimum competency/functional literacy variety. While varied in some ways, they all manifested a few common characteristics:

(i)   All were multiple choice in nature. In 'writing' tests, students actually wrote not a word but bubbled in a response on an IBM sheet.
(ii) The precepts of Latinate grammar, correct usage and rules of mechanics (capitalization, punctuation, spelling) were featured in the writing test.
(iii) No oral elements were included.
(iv) Elements of the writing process were seldom included.
(v)   They were created by psychometricians. Rarely was a linguist or rhetorician included in that creation process.
(vi) Remedial classes sprung into being for those students who failed; in fact much classroom instruction at the grade levels in question featured teaching to the test.
(vii) In one way or another, teachers' evaluations by their administrators were linked to test results.

Under some pressure from universities and professional organizations, Florida made a furtive attempt to add a 'Product Writing Test' to the established set of instruments. Using holistic scoring techniques taught to selected groups of high school English teachers, the state offered an assigned writing test component to a random sample of 10th grade groups in 1979. By 1981, the project was abandoned as being too clumsy and too costly to administer. The state of California made a more extensive and sophisticated effort to create a product writing test in the early 1990s. The project bogged down not because of inadequate funding but from opposition to composition topics raised by the Christian Right. In fall 1994, Republican Governor Pete Wilson vetoed that element of the testing package.

Meanwhile, citizens in many states expressed support for their testing programs throughout the 1970s and early 80s. They embraced that Scoreboard which appeared in local newspapers and on the 6 o'clock local evening TV news broadcasts. It was considered akin to a spelling contest or, better still, the results of the Friday night football games. They also expressed enthusiasm for the functional literacy tone of the test items. For most of their children, they reasoned, it was more important to read medicine labels, utility bills, or road maps than it was to respond to a Donne poem, a Hemingway novel, or an Ibsen play, or to express personal aspirations, concerns, or insights in writing. During this brief period of mild public advocacy, however, some other matters of national urgency began to emerge and to affect the sensibilities of the citizenry. These new matters would cause a whole panoply of educational reforms to be proposed — and the literacy 'question' could be found in the front ranks of these reforms.

Reagan, Bennett, Hirsch, and Cultural Catchup

In the USA, political developments invariably have a significant effect on the direction of public education. Sputnik influenced such changes. So did the Vietnam War and the urban uprisings of the late 60s and early 70s. The landslide election of Ronald Reagan to the presidency in November 1980 set in motion a true pendular swing in the manner in which literacy was perceived by educators nationwide. Along with Reagan's substantial victory, no fewer than six mainline liberal, senior US senators were unseated on that memorable night: Bayh of Indiana, Nelson of Wisconsin, Culver of Iowa, McGovern of South Dakota, Church of Idaho, and Magnuson of Washington. The election finally and wholly erased the programs of the Kennedy-Johnson years and led to the introduction of a new term in the education lexicon: cultural literacy.

The Reagan administration brought in a cadre of cultural elitists who set to work at once to do away with an educational philosophy dedicated to placing help for the less fortunate on the far back burner. Commissioner Terrel Bell immediately established a task force under John Gardner which, in 1981, produced a document titled *A Nation at Risk*. This report became required reading throughout the fifty states. It decried a nation's educational system 'drowning in a sea of mediocrity' and urged a rededication to the quest for 'excellence' in public school curricula. That report was followed in 1983 with a text edited by the esteemed former commissioner Ernest Boyer, underwritten by the Carnegie Foundation, and titled *High School*. As did the Gardner report, *High School* painted a picture of a minimum competency upper grade curriculum and called for the institution of high academic standards in the secondary schools of the nation.

As these reports were having their impact on the several state education establishments, Commissioner Bell was laying the groundwork for the cultural literacy. He appointed William Bennett to head the National Endowment for the Humanities (NEH). Armed with data from the second NAEP report, which reflected declining scores in reading, history, literature and writing (among others), Bennett began an intensive campaign to raise the cultural and intellectual levels of public school curricula, grades K-14. For this endeavor, he recruited a group of conservative academics: Diane Ravitch, Chester Finn, Lynn Cheney, and a Yale professor of hermeneutics named ED Hirsch, Jr.

Bennett was the senior author of the 1984 NEH pamphlet, *To Reclaim a Legacy*, whose main thrust was to reveal the dramatic decline in the academic content of high school programs of study. The thesis of all position papers emanating from the NEH in the early 80s was that the egalitarian minimum competency/ functional literacy apostles of the previous fifteen years had led to the near obliteration of curricula which introduced the cultural heritage of Western civilization to the youth of the country. The followers of Bell and Bennett related this decline to the downward spiral of US productivity and success on world economic markets; i.e., Japanese and West German business leaders had surpassed the Americans in their markets largely due to the vigorous curricula which they imposed on their children and adolescents.

Most states reacted to this philosophical reversal by passing legislation which mandated heightened academic programs and requirements for graduation. In Florida, for example, a bill was passed and signed into law which increased the number of academic courses a student must pass in order to graduate. It also increased the academic elements, for students who wished to enter the state's post-secondary institutions, must complete. Given the fact that a majority of high school students entered community junior colleges rather than four-year institutions, the new requirements caused great consternation; in the past, a high school diploma had been the only prerequisite to junior college admission. The Florida RAISE bill (Raise Achievement in Secondary Education) represented the new, elitist direction of US curricula.

In 1985, following Reagan's smashing re-election victory, William Bennett became US Commissioner of Education, and one of his lieutenants, Lynn Cheney, was elected to the NEH Director's position. (Ms Cheney is the wife of the then Secretary of Defense Richard Cheney; with the Clinton election in 1992, she was deposed and now serves as a conservative debater on CNN's usually vitriolic news commentary show *Crossfire*). To say that Ms Cheney carried on the Bennett crusade would be an understatement. Her NEH pamphlet *American Memory* (1986) provided a ringing denouncement of the cultural ignorance of American high school and college students. In the next year, the widely reputed scholar Allan Bloom published *The Closing of the American Mind*, whose thesis was that American higher education is failing its students because a politically oriented leadership had 'dumbed down' most liberal studies courses and did so to placate the strident voices of minority groups. Thus, to Bloom, the curriculum now pandered to the least able, least promising students and largely ignored or undervalued the probable intellectual, social, economic and political leaders of the future.

The text which most clearly reflects the academic movement of the 1980s, however, is ED Hirsch, Jr.'s *Cultural Literacy: What Every American Should Know* (1987). This book, one of the very few about education which ever made the best seller list, was written while its author was a member of the Bennett/Cheney staff. It elevated him to the role of cultural guru of US education and caused parent groups to form coast-to-coast, supporting his recipe for reform of the nation's schools.

In his *Preface*, Hirsch sounds the alarm voiced by several of the curricular critics already named in this chapter:

> To be culturally literate is to possess the basic information needed to thrive in the modern world. The breadth of that information is great, extending over the major domains of human activity from sports to science. It is by no means confined to 'culture' narrowly understood as an acquaintance with the arts. Nor is it confined to one social class. Quite the contrary, cultural literacy constitutes the only sure avenue of opportunity for disadvantaged children, the only reliable way of combating the social determinism that now condemns them to remain in the same social and educational condition as their parents. That children from poor and illiterate homes tend to remain poor and illiterate is an unacceptable failure of our schools, one which has occurred not because our teachers are inept but chiefly because they are compelled to teach a fragmented curriculum based on faulty educational theories. Some say that our schools by themselves are powerless to change the cycle of poverty and illiteracy. I do not agree. They can break the cycle, but only if they themselves break fundamentally with some of the theories and practices that education professors and school administrators have followed over the past fifty years. (p. xiii)

For Hirsch, the inculcation of the heritage must begin in early school years and continue through high school, at least for those who decide not to pursue their education further. In fact, he has stated the conviction that if the groundwork hasn't been substantially laid by grade 6 (age 11), no remedial work in upper grades could prove adequate. And, throughout the process, he insists on the need for considerable memorization to be demanded by all teachers and practiced by all students:

> Children also need to understand elements of our literary and mythic heritage that are often alluded to without explanation, for example, Adam and Eve, Cain and Abel, Noah and the Flood, David and Goliath, the Twenty-third Psalm, Humpty Dumpty, Jack Sprat, Jack and Jill, Little Jack Horner, Cinderella, Jack and the Beanstalk, Mary Had A Little Lamb, Peter Pan and Pinocchio. Also Achilles, Adonis, Aeneas, Agamemnon, Antigone and Apollo, as well as Robin Hood, Paul Bunyan, Satan, Sleeping Beauty, Sodom and Gomorrah, the Ten Commandments, and Tweedledum and Tweedledee. (*This author notes the peculiar juxtaposition of the Twenty-third Psalm and Humpty Dumpty, and Ten Commandments and Tweedledum and Tweedledee, albeit alphabetical.*)

> Our current distaste for memorization is more pious than realistic. At an early age when their memories are most retentive, children have an almost instinctive urge to learn specific tribal traditions. At that age

they seem to be fascinated by catalogues of information and are eager to master the materials that authenticate their membership in adult society. Observe for example how they memorize the rather complex materials of football, baseball, and basketball, even without benefit of formal avenues by which that information is inculcated. (*ibid.*, p. 30)

The memorization issue quickly became one of the most contentious to those who began to scrutinize Hirsch's manifesto. Another was the understandable suspicion that he was advocating a modern day elitism, as were his colleagues Bennett, Finn and Cheney (add to that list Boston University president, John Silber, who, in an earlier time, had been Bennett's mentor). To the 'elitist' and 'memorization charges', Hirsch had strong words:

Some have objected that teaching the traditional literate culture means teaching conservative material. Orlando Patterson answered that objection when he pointed out that mainstream culture is not the province of any single social group and is constantly changing by assimilating new elements and expelling old ones. Although mainstream culture is tied to the written word and may therefore seem more formal and elitist than other elements of culture, that is an illusion. Literate culture is the most democratic culture in our land: it excludes nobody; it cuts across generations and social groups and classes; it is not usually one's first culture, but it should be everyone's second, existing as it does beyond the narrow spheres of family, neighborhood, and region. (*ibid.*, p. 21)

After making the case for cultural literacy as the needed direction of US education, Hirsch offers some definitional perspective:

Having traced the nature of cultural literacy and shown its importance to national education, I want to consider the practical implications of the ideas I have set forth.

One immediate implication is that we have an obligation to identify and publish the contents of cultural literacy. It is reasonable to think that those contents can be identified explicitly, since they are identified implicitly by every writer or speaker who addresses the general public. If writers did not make tacit assumptions about the knowledge they could take for granted in their audiences, their writing would be so cumbersome as to defeat the aim of communication.

It is true that the specific content of the national literate vocabulary changes from year-to-year, even from day-to-day, as striking events catch national attention. But such changes are few when compared to the words and associations that stay the same. Of course, one literate person's sense of the shared national vocabulary is not precisely identical with another's; individual experiences produce different assumptions in different people about shared knowledge. But these differences

are insignificant compared to what is common in the systems of associations that we acquire by daily experiences of literate culture.

It's also true that we adapt our conjectures about what others
know to particular circumstances. Obviously, the knowledge we
assume when we talk to a young child is substantially different from
that which we take for granted in addressing an educated adult, and
we constantly make other adjustments to our audiences. But when we
address a general audience we must assume that we are addressing a
'common reader', that is, a literate person who shares with us a common body of knowledge and associations. Since we so frequently
have to posit a common reader in writing or public speaking, it should
be possible to reach a large measure of agreement about what the
common reader knows. (*ibid.*, pp. 134–5)

To actualize his curriculum, Hirsch developed over the next two years
two dictionaries, one for children, the other for young adults, which spelled
out the literary texts, the historical epochs, the geographic, the artistic and
musical masterpieces about which 'literate' Americans should have some knowledge. For the first two or three years, the dictionaries sold well; as this essay
is written however, they have largely disappeared from the shelves of commercial and university bookstores throughout the country. In 1990, Hirsch created the Cultural Literacy Foundation, with generous federal and private funds,
at the University of Virginia, where he holds an endowed chair in English.
In 1991, the first of his *Cultural Literacy Texts, Grades One-Six* was published
by Doubleday & Co. In fall of that year, an elementary school, Three Oaks,
Fort Myers, Florida, began implementation of his program. The Three Oaks
area of Fort Myers is largely white and affluent. Four years later, it is still using
the approach, although the curriculum has not been widely adopted in Florida
or elsewhere.

Thus, for a full decade, the spirit of cultural literacy flourished in the
United States. There were other portents on the horizon, however, which
would divert the dialogue on literacy in new and (to some) disturbing directions. And it is these perspectives on the issues of what literacy is and
how it can best be offered to students in American public schools with which
this essay will reach its culmination. The proposals, counter proposals, and
debates now to be described still preoccupy US educators and presumably
will do so into the immediate future, or, as the romantics would probably
intone, into the dawn of the new century.

Post Thesis — A Prophecy of Things to Come

Not surprisingly, the first to be considered is the ever increasingly powerful influence which modern technology wields over educational thought on
this side of the Atlantic. The immense and widespread power electronic

instruments would have on the industrialized world was meticulously and ominously foretold by Marshall McLuhan in his renowned 1964 text *Understanding Media*. Over the next quarter century, these media, especially commercial television, grew in craftsmanship, availability, and popular influence. During those years, only a few prophets warned us of the impending diminution of print in public discourse and in education. The most compelling and eloquent warnings of what the cathode tube had already bequeathed to our society and what probable directions it would follow were voiced by one of McLuhan's graduate students and ardent admirers, Dr. Neil Postman (New York University) in his text *Amusing Ourselves to Death* (1985). Postman's analysis provides a significant transition from the cultural literacy emphases to the overweening concern of the 1990s: that the pervasive stranglehold which TV now wields over American culture could well sound the death knell of reading (which he calls the 'typographic mind') and could lead this society into cultural catastrophe if its influences are not recognized and contested.

Rather than provide an extensive explication of this very important text (winner of the National Book Award for non-fiction in 1985), I choose to select a few excerpts from the book and briefly annotate them, in my belief that the messages in the passages chosen will be sufficiently relevant and affective. Postman (1985) sets the tone for his prophecy in the Foreword:

> We were keeping our eye on 1984. When the year came and the prophecy didn't, thoughtful Americans sang softly in praise of themselves. The roots of liberal democracy had held. Wherever else the terror had happened, we, at least, had not been visited by Orwellian nightmares.
>
> But we had forgotten that alongside Orwell's dark vision, there was another — slightly older, slightly less well known, equally chilling: Aldous Huxley's *Brave New World*. Contrary to common belief even among the educated, Huxley and Orwell did not prophesy the same thing. Orwell warns that we will be overcome by an externally imposed oppression. But in Huxley's vision, no Big Brother is required to deprive people of their autonomy, maturity and history. As he saw it, people will come to love their oppression, to adore the technologies that undo their capacities to think.
>
> What Orwell feared were those who would ban books. What Huxley feared was that there would be no reason to ban a book, for there would be no one who wanted to read one. Orwell feared those who would deprive us of information. Huxley feared those who would give us so much that we would be reduced to passivity and egoism. Orwell feared that the truth would be concealed from us. Huxley feared the truth would be drowned in a sea of irrelevance. Orwell feared we would become a captive culture. Huxley feared we would become a trivial culture, preoccupied with some equivalent of the feelies, the orgy porgy, and the centrifugal bumblepuppy. As Huxley

remarked in *Brave New World Revisited*, the civil libertarians and rationalists who are ever on the alert to oppose tyranny 'failed to take into account man's almost infinite appetite for distractions'. In *1984*, Huxley added, people are controlled by inflicting pleasure. In short, Orwell feared that what we hate will ruin us. Huxley feared that what we love will ruin us.

This book is about the possibility that Huxley, not Orwell, was right. (pp. vii–viii)

Having raised the Huxleyan warning, Postman, in his opening chapter, provides a symbolic view of American culture through a terse but dismaying series of three snapshots:

At different times in our history, different cities have been the focal point of a radiating American spirit. In the late eighteenth century, for example, Boston was the center of a political radicalism that ignited a shot heard round the world — a shot that could not have been fired any other place but the suburbs of Boston. At its report, all Americans, including Virginians, became Bostonians at heart. In the mid-nineteenth century, New York became the symbol of the idea of a melting-pot America — or at least a non-English one — as the wretched refuse from all over the world disembarked at Ellis Island and spread over the land their strange languages and even stranger ways. In the early twentieth century, Chicago, the city of big shoulders and heavy winds, came to symbolize the industrial energy and dynamism of America. If there is a statue of a hog butcher somewhere in Chicago, then it stands as a reminder of the time when America was railroads, cattle, steel mills and entrepreneurial adventures. If there is no such statue, there ought to be, just as there is a statue of a Minute Man to recall the Age of Boston, as the Statue of Liberty recalls the Age of New York.

Today, we must look to the city of Las Vegas, Nevada, as a metaphor of our national character and aspiration, its symbol a thirty-foot-high cardboard picture of a slot machine and a chorus girl. For Las Vegas is a city entirely devoted to the idea of entertainment, and as such proclaims the spirit of a culture in which all public discourse increasingly takes the form of entertainment. Our politics, religion, news, athletics, education and commerce have been transformed into congenial adjuncts of show business, largely without protest or even much popular notice. The result is that we are a people on the verge of amusing ourselves to death. (*ibid.*, pp. 3–4)

After contrasting the print medium, which reflects data and concepts through connected clusters of language with the electronic media, which does so with visual images, Postman devotes considerable discussion to 'typographic

America', primarily during the nineteenth and early twentieth centuries. It is his contention that while communication was conducted through oral and (more so) print means, America was at its intellectual zenith. Using the Lincoln-Douglas debates of the 1850s as his prime example, Postman contends that argument was truly joined and extended in that era and that much formal language, presented orally (as in the Debates) was 'pure print'. He concludes the review of that era with this statement:

> The name I give to that period of time during which the American mind submitted itself to the sovereignty of the printing press is the Age of Exposition. Exposition is a mode of thought, a method of learning, and a means of expression. Almost all of the characteristics we associate with mature discourse were amplified by typography, which has the strongest possible bias toward exposition: a sophistic-ated ability to think conceptually, deductively and sequentially: a high valuation of reason and order; an abhorrence of contradiction; a large capacity for detachment and objectivity; and a tolerance for delayed response. Toward the end of the nineteenth century, for reasons I am most anxious to explain, the Age of Exposition began to pass, and the early signs of its replacement could be discerned. Its replacement was to be the Age of Show Business. (*ibid.*, p. 63)

Moving to the center of his argument, Postman then describes the gradual but inexorable changes which the nineteenth century inventions of the telegraph and the photograph created in US culture. When the two were integrated to provide information to listeners/viewers in this country, the tempo of the change was greatly accelerated. He states, in a chapter titled 'The Peek-a-Boo World' that:

> In a peculiar way, the photograph was the perfect complement to the flood of telegraphic news-from-nowhere that threatened to submerge readers in a sea of facts from unknown places about strangers with unknown faces. For the photograph gave a concrete reality to the strange-sounding datelines, and attached faces to the unknown names. Thus it provided the illusion, at least, that 'the news' had a connection to something within one's sensory experience. It created an apparent context for the news of the day. And the 'news of the day' created a context for the photograph. (*ibid.*, p. 75)

He then moves quickly to the onset of television as the consummate off-spring of that wedding. He makes his feelings about the dramatic growth of this medium abundantly clear:

> Television has become, so to speak, the background radiation of the social and intellectual universe, the all-but-imperceptible residue

of the electronic big bang of a century past, so familiar and so thoroughly integrated with American culture that we no longer hear its faint hissing in the background or see the flickering gray light. This, in turn, means that its epistemology goes largely unknown. And the peek-a-boo world it has constructed around us no longer seems even strange.

There is no more disturbing consequence of the electronic and graphic revolution than this: that the world as given to us through television seems natural, not bizarre. For the loss of the sense of the strange is a sign of adjustment, and the extent to which we have adjusted is a measure of the extent to which we have been changed. Our culture's adjustment to the epistemology of television is by now all but complete; we have so thoroughly accepted its definitions of truth, knowledge and reality that irrelevance seems to us to be filled with import, and incoherence seems eminently sane. And if some of our institutions seem not to fit the template of the times, why is it they, and not the template, that seems to us disordered and strange. (*ibid.*, pp. 79–80)

The next five chapters serve to amplify the increasing and insuperable effects which all TV, but mostly the commercial variety, have had on American culture in general and literacy in particular. These chapters treat television and current interests, news reporting, religious involvement, political campaigns and education. While too much quoting may turn off some readers, I, as a professional educator of almost forty years could not resist including the opening lines from the chapter, 'Teaching as an Amusing Activity':

There could not have been a safer bet when it began in 1969 than that *Sesame Street* would be embraced by children, parents and educators. Children loved it because they were raised on television commercials, which they intuitively knew were the most carefully crafted entertainments on television. To those who had not yet been to school, even to those who had just started, the idea of being taught by a series of commercials did not seem peculiar. And that television should entertain them was taken as a matter of course.

Parents embraced *Sesame Street* for several reasons, among them that it assuaged their guilt over the fact that they could not or would not restrict their children's access to television. *Sesame Street* appeared to justify allowing a 4 or 5-year-old to sit transfixed in front of a television screen for unnatural periods of time. Parents were eager to hope that television could teach their children something other than which breakfast cereal had the most crackle. At the same time, *Sesame Street* relieved them of the responsibility of teaching their pre-school children how to read — no small matter in a culture where children are apt to be considered a nuisance. They could also plainly see that, in spite of its faults, *Sesame Street* was entirely consonant with the prevailing spirit of America. Its use of cute puppets, celebrities, catchy tunes, and rapid-fire editing was certain to give pleasure to the children and would therefore serve as adequate preparation for their entry into a fun-loving culture.

As for educators, they generally approved of *Sesame Street*, too. Contrary to common opinion, they are apt to find new methods congenial, especially if they are told that education can be accomplished more efficiently by means of the new techniques. (That is why such ideas as 'teacher-proof' textbooks, standardized tests, and, now, microcomputers have been welcomed into the classroom.) *Sesame Street* appeared to be an imaginative aid in solving the growing problem of teaching Americans how to read, while, at the same time, encouraging children to love school.

We now know that *Sesame Street* encourages children to love school only if school is like *Sesame Street*. Which is to say, we know that *Sesame Street* undermines what the traditional idea of school represents. Whereas a classroom is a place of social interaction, the space in front of a television set is a private preserve. Whereas in a classroom, one may ask a teacher questions, one can ask nothing of a television screen. Whereas school is centered on the development of language, television demands attention to images. Whereas attending school is a legal requirement, watching television is an act of choice. Whereas in school, one fails to attend to the teacher at the risk of punishment, no penalties exist for failing to attend to the television screen. Whereas to behave oneself in school means to observe rules of public decorum, television watching requires no such observances, has no concept of public decorum. Whereas in a classroom, fun is never more than a means to an end, on television it is the end in itself. (*ibid.*, p. 142)

The huge hi-tech conglomerates of today may be somewhat irked by the above analysis, but I can't imagine any thoughtful teacher not agreeing wholeheartedly.

Postman's final chapter, 'The Huxleyan Warning', begins with this ominous statement:

What Huxley teaches is that in the age of advanced technology, spiritual devastation is more likely to come from an enemy with a smiling face than from one whose countenance exudes suspicion and hate. In the Huxleyan prophecy, Big Brother does not watch us, by his choice. We watch him, by ours. There is no need for wardens or gates or Ministries of Truth. When a population becomes distracted by trivia, when cultural life is redefined as a perpetual round of entertainments, when serious public conversation becomes a form of baby-talk, when, in short, a people become an audience and their public business a vaudeville act, then a nation finds itself at risk; culture-death is a clear possibility. (*ibid.*, pp. 155–6)

Postman goes on to exhort his readers to establish a critical thinking/reading environment in their classrooms which will sound an alarm to young people and adults alike as to the dangerous encroachments which television has made and can make on all public discourse in the USA.

To the Present: Diversity and Technology *Uber Alles*

Postman's deep concern with the increasing influence of media technology, among other things, provides a kind of transition between the cultural literacy era and the high-tech multicultural guise which the literacy concepts have assumed in the first half of the twentieth century's last decade. Those two features, plus the 'reading-writing' connections now touted in much professional literature, reflect the literacy landscape of the present day.

Soon after establishing his Cultural Literacy Foundation, hard by the University of Virginia campus in 1990, Hirsch called together 100 literacy authorities from across the country. They met in Charlottesville, Virginia, in March of that year to critique his attempt to convert the theories in his 1987 text into curricular materials and teacher training paraphernalia subsequently to be exported to a small number of pilot schools; from thence they were to be disseminated nationwide. None of these authorities represented the major professional groups such as the Modern Language Association, NCTE, IRA, the Association for Supervision and Curriculum Development, etc. Hirsch was leery of input from such groups from the outset and has consistently refused to address their national gatherings.

After three days of intense dialogue, the group offered its host a number of suggestions for modification/addition to his construct. Of these, two seem quite prophetic, viewed across four-and-a-half years of retrospect:

(i) The 'cultural' concept must be broadened; i.e., in its 1987 dress, it was too 'Eurocentric'. Thus, before the meeting ended, Hirsch had appointed 'consultants' in four areas: women's studies, African-American studies, Hispanic studies, and Native American studies. (Needless to say, the two dictionaries were in need of immediate 'updating'.)

(ii) The process dimension of learning, one which was roundly excoriated in the text, was given a more influential role in the curricular system. Some ways of going about the teaching of reading and writing were urged of the Hirschian curriculum creators as they began their struggle to create a paradigm for grade 1 (6-year olds).

The demand for (i) above would have come as no surprise to anyone who had been following political, social, cultural, and their resulting curricular trends over the past forty years or so. In one sense, it reflects a broader concern found both in society and in certain enclaves of US educational leadership: the distrust of and outright hostility toward tradition. To many modern-day critics, this term has provided an umbrella which covers the study of dead white male authors, to emphasis on formal elements of the English grammar (for example, Latinate grammar and 'correct' usage), to reading just about anything encased in a *book* with *pages* of *print*, to formulaic writing (for example, the five paragraph theme) on white, lined paper, by pencil or ballpoint pen. More particularly, the pressure is on educators to review current curricular offerings which, in the protestors' eyes, are far too Eurocentric in emphasis. As is usually the case in the USA, the clearly multicultural movement began in California. The 1978 legislature in the Golden State passed a bill which, among other things, mandated the presence of more female, Hispanic, African-American, Native American (Indian), and Asiatic persons, communities, events, and lifestyle elements to *any* curricular materials which would be adopted and paid for by the state.

During the past ten years or so, this type of influence on what students are assigned, or even permitted to read, has intensified. The sobriquet, 'political correctness' is an all too familiar label associated with those who are aggressively and intensively liberal in their opposition to the presence of anything 'offensive' in school curricula.

Who are these politically correct critics? What do they want? Where have they come from? And how have they influenced American culture in general and the public school students' right to read, in particular? Probably the most clearly discernible antecedents of today's left-wing challenges can be found among the Civil Rights activists of the 1950s and 60s. In those ranks could be counted a large number of college-age individuals, of both genders, for whom the battle to integrate all facilities and institutions in the Deep South was only the main thrust in their goal, which was to expose, to question, to attack, and ultimately to dispose of the status quo. The most heralded struggles — Little Rock Central High School (1957), James Meredith's entrance into Ole Miss (1962), and George Wallace's stand before the registrar's office at University of Alabama (1963) — suggest that these young, liberal-minded crusaders viewed American education as a significant item on their agenda.

The Civil Rightists were joined in the late 60s and 70s by other groups whose agendas went far beyond the elimination of Jim Crow in the states of the Old Confederacy. The Hippies with their lyrical leaders (Bob Dylan, Joan Baez, etc.) set about to reform America. Their most distinctive opponents (and scapegoats) were the white males of The Establishment who seemed to these young activists to be the cause of the country's most diabolical problems: the perpetuation of the Vietnam War, the deterioration of the environment, the miserable living conditions of the inner cities and the oppression of the minorities. This expanded focus took in additional individuals and groups whose names have also become familiar if not legendary in this quarter century.

Since the publication of his 1960s book, *Unsafe at Any Speed*, Ralph Nader has become a cult figure among consumer advocates and environmentalists, two more groups now agitating for change in the system. Moreover, the push for equal rights inevitably took on the modern day suffragettes whose earlier title, women's libbers, has given way to the feminist label, circa 1993. One of the deeper concerns of this latter group, besides passage of the Equal Rights amendment, and enforcement of Title IX of the Civil Rights Act, has been the place of women in the public education hierarchy, the number of female authors studied in literature programs, and the stereotypes of female characters in texts widely taught, all the way from Cinderella to graduate fiction seminars at Harvard, Chicago, Berkeley and elsewhere.

The cursory description of the Equal Rights movements of the past half century (it has, after all, been over fifty years since the African-American baseball player, Jackie Robinson, was hired by the Brooklyn Dodgers) rendered above has had a marked effect on materials choices in all curricular areas and at all grade levels in this inclusive time span. In 1964, the Illinois chapter of the NAACP (National Association for the Advancement of Colored People) forced the removal of *The Adventures of Huckleberry Finn* from the state's schools, citing as its rationale the negative image of character Nigger Jim. The same objection was raised by a number of parents in Bucks County, Pennsylvania, some twenty years later, also causing the renowned Twain novel to be temporarily removed. This particular issue continues among black activists as this is written. While the Bucks County conflict was raging, the National Organization of Women (NOW) forced the cancellation of a Broadway production of *Lolita*, citing the compromised image of females as their rationale.

Spokespersons for other minority groups, chief among them Hispanics, Native Americans and Asiatics, joined forces with the groups noted above and began, among other things, to question the choice of text offerings used in the schools, particularly those which ignored minority considerations or placed representative characters from such groups in pejorative roles. The upshot of this burgeoning concern with the status and image of women, minorities, and citizens' groups such as the environmentalists, was to influence the use or exclusion of certain materials and authors from the curriculum. They also urged the addition of new selections to revised anthologies. Harried publishers, long confronted by apostles of the right wing (especially fundamentalist Christians), now began to feel pressure from the New Left coalition. The recent addition to pressure groups of the gay-lesbian community has added to the turmoil. In a December 1981 *English Journal* piece titled 'Proactive censorship: The new wave', I took note of these doings:

> Today, when writing a book for use in public schools, an author must be aware of:

1   how many black faces appear in proportion to the number of white faces;
2   the use of names such as Carlos and Juanita in proportion to those of Billy and Sue;
3   the use of pronouns that *negate* sex bias;
4   putting anyone in a stereotypical role;
5   paying obeisance to mandates of the consumer enlightenment moguls;
6   excluding materials that imply the rape of our natural beauty;
7   any vaguely humorous, satiric, and/or critical treatment of anyone's religious preference;
8   any allusion to stereotypes of ethnic or national origins;
9   statements that may contain political bias;
10 references to the use of drugs, tobacco, alcohol, non-nutritious foods, etc. (Simmons, 1981, p. 19)

Little did I realize that this was truly the tip of the iceberg.

Thus the multiculturalists have made, and continue to make their assault on US programs of study at *all* levels. (The battle of text choice in college English departments has reached fever pitch.) In doing so, they seem determined to rewrite the concept of literacy, at least in terms of scope of texts and issues. As this is written, communities and campuses across the country have been sensitized to the conflicts. Many are providing input, usually acrimonious, in a number of forums.

Another, less confrontational, direction taken by those who would at least modify more traditional views of literacy is being taken by those theorists and classroom practitioners who are promoting the 'reading-writing connection'. To these educators, whose primary focus is on the early schooling years (kindergarten through grade 5; ages 4–10), this is hardly an innovative happening. They have been urging the adoption of integrated language arts activities — now called by some whole language teaching — for over seventy years. The emergence of the middle school in the late 60s, however, has caused followers of reading-writing instructional paradigms to focus their argument on higher grade levels. Middle schools, developed initially to cope with exploding student populations and widespread racial integration, have grown farther and farther apart from the junior high schools, which, by 1995, they have largely replaced coast-to-coast. The latter schools offered curricula which by and large imitated those of senior high counterparts. Thus, subject matter was rigidly compartmentalized, content focus was the name of the game, and new teachers emanated from secondary rather than elementary training programs.

Once the administrative kinks had been largely straightened out, however, a whole new curricular spirit began to arise among the middle schools' leaders. It was heavily student-centered in emphasis and featured integration rather than separation of subject matter components. Thus reading courses, once entities unto themselves, and usually remedial in thrust, became increasingly

joined with English, social studies and even science offerings. Given this cooperative spirit, it is little wonder that proposals to combine reading and writing
instruction began to appear. Separate reading instruction had often amounted
to an endless series of journeys through sterile, rigidly sequential workbook
exercises. What the youngsters were reading about as they plowed through
their fill-in-the-blank ordeal was almost never related to their backgrounds,
needs, or interests. Similarly, writing instruction, until very recently in the hands
of the grammar apostles and the rhetorical-model freaks (write a five-sentence
paragraph introduced by a topic sentence and followed by three sentences,
each containing one supporting detail and ended with a clincher sentence[4]),
began to move in a new, emancipated direction.

The writings of James Moffett, which first attracted attention in the late
60s, directed attention to classroom work featuring the integration of the
language capacities of children and youth. In *Teaching the Universe of Discourse* (1968) Moffett called for a wholesale restructuring of classroom instruction based largely on the language learning theories of Piaget and Vygotsky.
His companion text, *Student Centered Language Arts, K-12*, was published in
the same year. Both attracted admiration and attention by university theorists
but were largely either overlooked or spurned by the teaching rank and file.
The suggestions, at the time, seemed too radical, and the texts emerged just
as those teachers were feeling the lash of State Education Department mandates bent on Accountability.

By the late 80s, however, a different environment had been shaped. Nancie
Atwell, an 8th grade English teacher in Boothbay Harbor, Maine, published *In
the Middle* (1988), a text based heavily on classroom research conducted by
the author herself. It lays out an original outline of reading — writing collabor-
ative instruction in which the students become partners with each other and
the teacher as they seek to understand and compose meaningful discourse.
Atwell's classroom-as-workshop model has caught on in middle schools nationwide. Her text is probably as widely used in English methods courses as any
currently in print. It would be hard to imagine a National Writing Project institute which did not include the text near the top of its required reading list. It
has certainly outlasted the Hirsch book in popularity and influence although
they were published in the same year. Rich with specific classroom strategies,
mini-lessons and dialogues, it continues to be a big-time seller as we colonists
head for the twenty-first century.

There may be more than coincidence in the fact that Ms Atwell hails
from a community in Maine. The last fifteen years have seen the rise of a new,
progressive, and highly touted center for the teaching of writing at the neighboring University of New Hampshire. Here, such gurus as Donald Murray and
Donald Graves have set up shop, attracting numbers of graduate students
and generous amounts of external funds to their operation. At roughly the
same time, a well known English education publishing house, Boynton-Cook,
became amalgamated with the Heinemann company. Located in Portsmouth,
New Hampshire, this publisher has produced the lion's share of professional

literature on the teaching of English over the past ten years, several texts of which have been written by members of the Murray-Graves camp. In 1983, James Moffett provided an influential text to the Portsmouth house, *Active Voices*, devoted to the concept of cooperative writing instruction, and now in its second edition. In 1992, a University of New Hampshire graduate and middle school teacher (Durham, N.H.) named Linda Rief produced *Seeking Diversity*, once again based on ten years of teaching and observation of middle schoolers' literacy learning styles. Rief has integrated the conclusions drawn from her classroom experiences with the theories of Atwell, Murray, Graves, Lucy Calkins, Ken and Yetta Goodman *et al.* Featuring further exploitation of the integration theory, this book has nearly rivaled the popularity of *In the Middle* with English educators and classroom teachers alike.

In 1992, Peter Elbow and Sheridan Blau, two highly capable teacher/researchers, with the help of Arthur Applebee and Judith Langer, produced a secondary level English series titled *Writer's Craft* (MacDougal-Littell) which represents the embodiment of the reading-writing connection for students in upper grades (grades 9–12). Beginning each instructional unit with a high-interest reading selection, they moved students into the implementation of the writing process and added a grammar/usage/mechanics component for assistance in revision of drafted compositions. The initial popularity of this series provides some evidence of the impact student-centered, integrated instruction in literacy is having on adolescents and their teachers at this time.

The final dimension of literacy in US schools to be noted has been labelled by most observers computer literacy. While the past decade has seen a dramatic increase in computer presence in American schools, as well as other electronic instructional marvels, the idea of technologically augmented instruction is hardly new around here. In the fabled 60s, a respected educational theorist named John Goodlad was writing books and speaking across the country on the promise of computer-assisted instruction. Interest in the use of videotape in teacher education was also on the upswing back then, and economy-minded educational futurists were proclaiming the potential of electronic media both to heighten students' interest in classroom tasks and to reduce some of the more repetitive clerical duties teachers were mandated to assume.

The big surge came, however, in the mid-80s when MacIntosh began to display to the world simple, compact, relatively inexpensive personal computers. Soon, one large conglomerate after another began to jump on the computer production band wagon, and school districts throughout the country were besieged with high-tech sales reps eager to demonstrate to district officials, school boards, and building principals the unavoidable truth that they had in their sample cases — the wave of the future.

There is a certain irony in the current 'Computers: A must for our schools' frenzy: American school systems in the 90s have faced increasingly tighter budgets. State support has dwindled; many states look to lottery receipts just to keep schools *open*. American taxpayers, led by the Ross Perots, Phil Gramms and Newt Gingriches of this world, vote down local referenda for their schools consistently. The new Republican congressional majority has cut deeply into federal support and threatens to close down the US Department of Education. State legislatures throughout the country are far more committed to building new prisons and designing execution chambers than they are to supporting their schools, at *all* levels. And in the wake of the financial picture, there is a great hue and cry across the land to bedeck every classroom with wall-to-wall computers. To some administrators, just having them in the room represents a status symbol — like a fleet of new buses or a refurbished gymnasium. I have observed in my frequent school visits large numbers of computers going unused, and this sense of waste has been corroborated by numerous colleagues when we converse at national meetings.

The will to achieve computer literacy, however, grows in the thinking of the nation's schools. Computer laboratories appear where libraries (now commonly called media centers) experience ever-shrinking new acquisitions for stocking their shelves and, not unexpectedly, the students get sucked in. True to Postman's prophecy, many middle and high school students will read materials on a computer screen while they balk at reading print materials. The *appearance* of growing computer literacy in US schools is everywhere, much to the joy of the high-tech titans whose Wall Street ratings go up and up.

It is fair to say, however, that actual development of computer-oriented instruction in English classrooms is still in the embryonic stage. Some teachers content themselves with introducing the equipment and having the students peck out a few lines on virtually *any* topic. Others have found the computer a helpful resource in the handing out of that senior high task, the research paper. In that endeavor, students are being either encouraged or mandated to seek resources in their libraries and in community, state, and even national repositories. In teaching writing, teachers demand (where equipment is available) that students outline, draft, and revise on their computers before submitting final products. And then there is that great contemporary savior, the spellchecker.

Some teachers of English and humanities courses have turned to the CD Rom as a regular instructional tool in assigning work in literary texts, art objects, and musical masterpieces. Interestingly, such equipment exists to a far greater extent in suburban schools than in inner-city or small, rural ones. Thus the socioeconomic gap grows even wider as we move deeper into the computer age.

Where the multicultural influences, the reading-writing synapses, and the high-tech additions will take us into the final half of the 1990s is anybody's guess. It is fair to say, however, that what is termed literacy at the dawn of the new century will bear little resemblance to what it was when the GIs returned to their American hometowns in 1945 and 1946. As an old American saying intones, 'You win some; you lose some'. As a long-time educator steeped in the traditions of reading critically, sharing quality literature, expressing significant ideas and perspectives in composed written statements, and withal, examining the human experience through print, I am somewhat sceptical of what is coming next. There are always younger colleagues who will quite probably supply comments on the need for dinosaurian hangers-on to retire to the nearest nursing home. Maybe they're right. In any case, it has been an extraordinary roller coaster ride.

Notes

1   This organization was created in 1911 and had from the onset been antagonistic to classical, elitist public school curricula.
2   A National Education Association text (1944) which provided a comprehensive treatise on education as affecting community living, vocational competence, citizenship, etc.
3   'The Basic Issue in the Teaching of English', supplement to *English Journal*, September 1959, pp. 19–20.
4   Author's Note: After thirty-eight years in the profession, I still don't have a clear notion of what a clincher sentence is.

References

American Collegiate Dictionary (1959) (CP Barnhart Ed.) New York, Random House.
APPLEBEE, A.N. (1974) *Tradition and Reform in the Teaching of English: A History*, Urbana, Il, NCTE.
ATWELL, N. (1987) *In the Middle*, Portsmouth, NH, Heinemann, Boynton-Cook.
Becoming a Nation of Readers (1984) The Report of the Commission on Reading, Washington, DC, National Institute of Education.
BENNETT, W. (1984) *To Reclaim a Legacy*, Washington, DC, National Endowment for the Humanities.
BESTOR, A. (1953) *Educational Wastelands*, Urbana, Il, University of Illinois Press.
BLOOM, A. (1987) *The Closing of the American Mind*, New York, Simon & Schuster.
BOYER, E.L. (1983) *High School: A Report on Secondary Education in America*, New York, Harper & Row.
BRITTON, J., SHAFER, R.E. and WATSON, K. (Eds) (1990) *Teaching and Learning English Worldwide*, Clevedon, Multilingual Matters Ltd.
BROENING, A.M. (Ed.) (1939) *Conducting Experiences in English, National Council of Teachers of English, Monograph #8*, New York, Appleton-Century-Crofts, Inc.
BRUNER, J. (1960) *The Process of Education*, Cambridge, MA, Harvard University Press.
CHENEY, L. (1986) *American Memory*, Washington, DC, National Endowment for the Humanities.
DEWEY, J. (1938) *Experience and Education*, New York, Collier.
DIXON, J. (1975) *Growth Through English*, London, Cox & Wyman Ltd.
EAGLESON, R.D. (Ed.) (1982) *English in the Eighties*, Adelaide, Australian Association for the Teaching of English.
Education for All American Youth (1944) National Education Association, Washington, DC, NEA.

ELBOW, P.B. and SHERIDAN B. (1992) *The Writer's Craft: Ideas to Expression*, Evanston, Il, McDougal-Littell Co.

FOGARTY, D.S.J. (1959) *Roots for a New Rhetoric*, New York, Teachers College Columbia University Press.

GOODLAD, J. (1966) *The Changing School Curriculum*, New York, McGraw Hill.

Freedom and Discipline in English (1965) College Entrance Examination Board. New York, CEEB.

HATFIELD, W.W. (1935) *An Experience Curriculum in English*, New York, Appleton Century Crofts.

HIRSCH, E.D., Jr. (1987) *Cultural Literacy: What Every American Needs to Know*, Boston, MA, Houghton Mifflin Co.

HIRSCH, E.D., Jr. (1988) *The Dictionary of Cultural Literacy: What Every American Needs to Know*, Boston, MA, Houghton Mifflin Co.

HIRSCH, E.D., Jr. (1989) *A First Dictionary of Cultural Literacy: What Our Children Need to Know*, Boston, MA, Houghton Mifflin Co.

KAESTLE, C.F. (1991) *Literacy in the United States*, New Haven, CT, Yale University Press.

KIERNAN, A. (1990) *The Death of Literature*, New Haven, CT, Yale University Press.

LYNCH, J. and BERTRAND E. (1963) *High School English Textbooks: A Critical Examination*, Boston, MA, Atlantic-Little & Brown.

LYND, A. (1953) *Quackery in the Public Schools*, Boston, MA, Little, Brown.

MALONEY, H. (Ed.) (1972) *Accountability and the Teaching of English*, Urbana, Il, NCTE.

MANDEL, B.J. (Ed.) (1980) *Three Language-Arts Curriculum Models*, Urbana, Il, NCTE.

McLUHAN, M. (1964) *Understanding Media: The Extensions of Man*, New York, The New American Library.

MOFFETT, J. (1968) *Teaching the Universe of Discourse*, Boston, MA, Houghton Mifflin Co.

MOFFETT, J. (1983) *Active Voice*, Portsmouth, NH, Heinemann, Boynton-Cook.

MOFFETT, J. and WAGNER, B.J. (1984) *Student-Centered Language Arts and Reading* (3rd ed.) Portsmouth, NH, Heinemann, Boynton-Cook.

A Nation at Risk (1981) National Commission on Excellence in Education. Washington, DC, US Dept. of Education.

National Assessment of Educational Progress Newsletter (1975) Education Commission of the States, Denver, NAEP.

PATTISON, R. (1982) *On Literacy*, Oxford, Oxford University Press.

POSTMAN, N. (1985) *Amusing Ourselves to Death*, New York, Penguin Books Inc.

RAVITCH, D. (1983) *The Troubled Crusade: US Education, 1945–1980*, New York, Basic Books Inc.

REICH, R.B. (1991) *The Work of Nations*, New York, Vintage Books.

RIEF L. (1992) *Seeking Diversity*, Portsmouth, NH, Heinemann, Boynton-Cook.

SHUGRUE, M.F. (1968) *English in a Decade of Change*, New York, Pegasus.

SIMMONS, J.S. (1981) 'Proactive censorship: The new wave', *English Journal*, Dec.

SIMMONS, J.S. (1994) *Censorship: A Threat to Reading, Learning, Thinking*, Newark, Del, International Reading Association.

SIMMONS, J.S. and DELUZAIN, H.E. (1992) *Teaching Literature in Middle and Secondary Grades*, Boston, MA, Allyn & Bacon Inc.

SMITH, D.V. (1941) *Communication, The Miracle of Shared Living*, New York, MacMillan Co.

SMITH, F. (1986) *Understanding Reading* (3rd ed.) Hillsdale, NJ, Lawrence Erlbaum Associates.

SMITH, M. (1949) *And Madly Teach*, Chicago, IL, Henry Regnery Co.

STONE, G.W. (1961) *Issues, Problems and Approaches in the Teaching of English*, New York, Holt Rinehart and Winston.

Webster's Ninth New Collegiate Dictionary (1987) Springfield, MA, Merriam-Webster Inc.

WILLINSKY, J. (1988) *The Well-Tempered Tongue: The Politics of Standard English in the High School*, New York, Teachers College Press.

2 Beyond England's National Curriculum for English

Ed Marum

Introduction

Recent years have seen the introduction of a National Curriculum for state schools in England and Wales. There is already a considerable body of literature on the subject (I include some details of this literature in the references following this chapter). The curriculum proposals have been introduced in stages for different age groups of children and for different subjects of the curriculum. Their introduction has been complicated by a continuing series of revisions and amendments made by successive Secretaries of State for Education during the 1990s. The most recent version of the proposals went through Parliament ('the new orders') in January, 1995, and came into effect from September 1995 for pupils in Key Stages 1 to 3 (pupils of 5 years of age to pupils of 14 years of age). The new orders for pupils in Key Stage 4 (14–16-year-olds) come into effect a year later, that is in September 1996. The National Curriculum proposals have entailed considerable changes both to the curriculum which is to be taught in schools and to the methods of assessment schools must use to monitor that curriculum.

None of this will be news to those in England who have been involved in school development, for they have seen over the past seven years perhaps more curricular alterations than they have witnessed since at least the 1960s. Such developments may, however, be of real interest to educationists working in the USA and in Europe for, I believe, they will see some interesting parallels to developments in their own countries over recent years. John Simmons and Bjørg Gundem (chapters 1 and 3 in this volume), for example, provide considerable food for reflection in their analyses of national developments: their discussions of two very different state systems bear a number of similarities to the situation which continues to develop in England. I shall come back to this point in chapter 8.

In England, teachers of English have seen more changes in their subject than most of their colleagues. Partly this has been because English as a subject has always generated wide and public attention in general social, political and media arenas. The most recent changes which have been introduced into

English teaching have again gained national attention in the media and have generated heated debates of a broader cultural nature, as well as the usual political, social and educational kind. Recent years have seen, for example, strikes and other industrial action being taken by teachers' unions, as well as some very vociferous opposition to the arrangements for the new testing which has accompanied the revised curriculum, particularly the new curriculum for English. The net result of all these changes may be summarized by saying that, in general terms, the teacher's position has been weakened, and a more centralized and 'conservative' state curriculum has been implemented by statute. There is an analysis of the changes in English teaching in Marum (1995). For the present, I shall quote only my view that —

> The revised orders for English in the National Curriculum represent the latest phase of an awkward, misconceived and politically-bungled attempt to achieve 'compromise' against the social and political contextual background of Britain in the 1990s, at a time when the Government is defensive on broad political fronts and understandably feels vulnerable to both internal and external criticisms. As a basis for policy, the orders are defunct: as an expression of a coherent view of 'literacy' they are lamentable; as a blueprint for the future, they are worthless. In so far as they give expression to any 'version' of English that might be so-called, they are backward-looking, regressive and extraordinarily partial in character. They fail to provide clear guidance for those involved in teaching English; they offer no vision for the future to those who are training to become English teachers and, above all, they fail to address the interests and needs of our young people. (pp. 47–8)

Unfortunately, the latest curriculum proposals for English can be seen as only the most recent example in a long line of policy-making statements, accompanied by implementation guidelines, which have characterized the history and development of the subject in the state school system. In this sense, the National Curriculum is a contemporary example, one in a long historical series, of imposed curricular frameworks for English which have appeared from time to time, which are implemented in law, if not always in common practice, and which to date have failed to win the hearts and minds of the teachers and pupils who are instructed to follow them. Such policy statements traditionally, therefore, have a relatively short-term social and political, as well as educational, existence. (For an intelligent review of historical policy development in English viewed from a sociopolitical perspective see Goodson and Medway, 1990.) Despite this, policy statements do of course have important implications for schools and for the young people who follow the programmes of study which are laid down for them. The professional 'consultation' process which was set up in order to gauge reactions to the National Curriculum proposals itself raises a host of questions, among them whether the 'consultation' was ever more than a paper exercise undertaken for public relations reasons. In the case of English, we are told in the report on the consultation process that it involved ten 'English-specific sessions' as 'part of the national launches in May'; additionally, there were seven workshop conferences for teachers held in June; further meetings were also held between professional officers for English with teachers and advisers; there were also 'consultation meetings' with a range of associations (School Curriculum and Assessment Authority, 1994). In addition, there were also 6681 responses to the consultation questionnaire and written comments were received from 'individuals, schools and others'.

Given all of this, it seems more than surprising that the report on the consultation process contains less than eight lines on media education, less than four lines on drama and less than five lines on information technology, since, prior to the 'consultation', the relative neglect of these three areas in the National Curriculum proposals had been amongst the profession's most serious concerns. Within the report, language is used to obscure rather than to clarify. For example, it contains statements such as the following: 'about a third of respondents felt that the proposals contained too little reference to media'; 'respondents felt that there was too little reference to drama'; 'nearly a third of respondents overall thought that there was insufficient emphasis on information technology, with this view strengthening in the later stages'. If the mandatory lists of authors to be studied in literature at Key Stages 3 and 4 (11–16-year-olds) were 'thought to be too prescriptive by over half of respondents', then what are the grounds for retaining such a specified list after 'revision'? (*ibid.*). No attempt is made to differentiate between the character of the numerous responses received; there is no indication at all that policy on English is an issue that might be openly discussed on the basis of argument. Above all, I believe the procedures involved and the nature of the 'consultation' undertaken display on the government's part, as well as on that of its officers, a profound insecurity of position and a real unwillingness to respond openly to the profession's genuine concerns.

In an obvious sense, none of this might be thought surprising, given the overtly political nature of the government's position and its real fear of the organized 'English' response within the education profession, which has also included support from large numbers of parents and school governors. What is perhaps more worrying, however, than even all of this, is the way in which literature has been prescribed within the revised orders for English and the effect that this will have on children in schools. At this point I should like to move away from my concerns with the National Curriculum *per se*, and into slightly different territory, in order to begin to outline my sense of the more general social context which I feel is important to an understanding of the relationship between literacy and the National Curriculum proposals for English. This social context has, I believe, considerable significance for the ways in which we need to address literacy in future.

Literature and Literacy

The revised orders for English in the National Curriculum include requirements regarding the types of literature to be studied at different stages of the
school curriculum. For 11–16-year-olds, for example, there is a requirement to
study Shakespeare and pre-twentieth century literature alongside other literature categories. This study is assessed by newly developed national tests at
14 and by revised public examinations at 16, as well as by teachers in schools.
Predictably, there has been considerable debate about the content of, and
cultural assumptions behind, the literature selected for study. The language
of the document betrays its provenance in such phrases as 'pupils should be
introduced to major works of literature from the English literary heritage in
previous centuries'. The 'exemplary' dramatists listed for study by secondary
pupils are all male. In poetry, there is a requirement to read 'poems of high
quality by four major poets, whose works were published before 1900'. Pupils
are to be 'given opportunities to . . . appreciate the characteristics that distinguish literature of high quality' and 'appreciate the significance of texts whose
language and ideas have been influential'. The three examples provided in the
latter category are 'Greek myths, the authorised version of the Bible, Arthurian
legends' (DES, 1995).

I think it is clear that all this speaks for itself. The issue of how such
an approach to literature can be reconciled with a multiracial, pluralist cultural perspective has not been addressed. There are clear echoes here of the
'nationalist' strand of cultural thinking that Gundem finds in recent Norwegian
developments (chapter 3 in this volume). Aside from the marginalization of
non-verbal literacies, there are broader issues arising from an implicit version
of literacy which takes very little account of wider media, information technology, other cultural forms, and the wider literacy environment generally. For
pupils, however, the issues are even sharper than this, educated as they have
been in a multiliterate global environment in which the printed book no longer
has a central position for many. Neil Campbell's forceful exploration of this
issue (chapter 6 in this volume) builds in part on our contemporary experience
of university students, for many of whom a book-based approach to literacy
is already obsolescent. We need to remember, moreover, that these students
passed through the English school system *before* the National Curriculum took
effect in the senior years of secondary school.

In part, of course, the book experience of pupils in school might help
explain their attitudes to what they read and influence the amount of reading that they do. In this context it is interesting to read a recent SCAA publication which provides a snapshot of what pupils in schools were reading
during one week in 1995 (SCAA, 1995). Among the findings of this report are
the following:

> The range and nature of class reading changed dramatically between
> year 3 (8-year-olds) and year 11 (16-year-olds). The reduction in the

number of books read higher up the school might be expected as more full-length texts are read. The reduction in the number of classes reading in each category, however, is less easily explained. Overall, the amount of wider reading recorded reduced as pupils' ages increased, and little reading of texts from other cultures and traditions was recorded.

The number of authors of modern fiction read fell from one hundred and thirty two to twenty-seven. The breadth of reading at the beginning of Key Stage 2 had, by year 11, become totally geared towards GCSE (General Certificate of Secondary Education Examination) requirements . . .

By year 11, reading had become increasingly orientated towards examinations. Set texts were being read, including rather more poetry than in year 8. There was evidence of considerable reliance on the anthologies provided by the GCSE boards. Little wider reading, reading of pre-1900 fiction or texts from other cultures and traditions, took place in this term . . .

The range of individual reading narrowed as pupils entered Key Stage 3, and by year 11 individual reading had almost entirely given way to the reading of set examination texts . . .

Year 11 teachers' responses to the question on individual reading, such as 'unknown' and 'not done in school time', suggest that, as pupils move up the school, independent reading is not perceived to be the school's concern. The programme of study for reading at Key Stages 2, 3 and 4 makes independent reading a requirement. This survey raises questions about the adequacy of book selection, monitoring and record keeping related to individual as well as to class reading. (pp. 10–20)

Aside from the issues arising from the influence of examinations on pupils' attitudes to reading, there are others raised here; to do with the degree of knowledge teachers have about pupils' actual reading, whether individual or otherwise; to do with the systems in use, other than memory, to record development in pupils' reading experience; to do with the curricular and administrative workloads imposed on teachers with large groups; to do with what are 'reasonable' expectations in classroom situations, and so on. While such a snapshot of evidence cannot supply the necessary answers, and given that it will be several years before any reliable data emerge from the post-National Curriculum English experience, there are few grounds here for complacency.

There is also the larger question of reading: if some teachers do not know what pupils read, on what basis do they make judgments about pupils' responses to literature, given the complexity of the task? Janssen and Rijlaarsdam (chapter 5 in this volume) go on to examine this territory in more detail and their work demands that further research in the area be regarded as a matter of priority for our better understanding of developing response to narrative. Having said this, over recent years our knowledge of pupils' response to literature has already been strengthened by a body of valuable work which will help contextualize other points I wish to make. For this reason, I shall now go on to discuss briefly the importance of this work, as I see it, in terms of what we now know, in cultural terms, about the relationship of literature to literacy.

There have been two works in particular which have been important in shaping my own understanding of the relationship between culture and response. The first is Fry (1985) and the second Sarland (1991). Both have made important points concerning the reading of young people and their discussions of that reading as part of their broader experience. For the present, I hope it will be sufficient to adopt Sarland's definition of 'culture' for my own purposes, as I try to develop an argument as to the ways in which we need to approach literacy issues now and in future:

> My use of the word 'culture' will . . . seem loose to some, as I talk of 'girls' culture', 'male culture', 'adolescent culture' and so on. Others may enter into the debate about whether what I am referring to is a culture, a sub-culture, or whatever. What I am concerned with is the making of meaning and value, the sharing of knowledge, opinion and prejudice, and the delineation of a shared emotional response to the world and its artefacts. It is this that I assume culture to be and I shall use the word as and when seems appropriate. (p. 2)

It is with the 'making of meaning and value' that I am concerned here. Both Fry and Sarland have shown that pupils' literary experience is not bounded by school. If one were to try to make judgments on the scope and range of children's reading, one could not do so without having regard to their experience outside school. In other words, the meaning and value professional educators ascribe to the reading of literature, and the cultural assumptions they make about the relative value of particular literary experiences, are often grounded in value systems which are not only in many respects clearly at odds with those of young people, but are moreover often based on a liberal, 'book-based' approach to culture which has been, for many of the younger generation, already superseded by more recent advances in our understanding of what 'literacy' is in society. Thus 'literature' tends to have connotations of status or 'high quality' (as the National Curriculum puts it) which is in practice at odds with the everyday assumptions and understandings of those who, by choice, read 'non-quality' literature but who gain, by so doing, a valuable learning experience not always possible when reading someone else's choice of book, whatever 'quality' it may be argued to possess. Ours is a society of multiliteracies, and no longer a society of the print-based culture which the printing press brought about. Therefore, while it is interesting and informative to hear from the SCAA that the survey previously referred to 'raises questions about the adequacy of book selection, monitoring and record keeping' of English teachers, some of the more important questions we might ask about the relationship of school-based reading experience to non school-based reading experience are forgotten. The implicit assumption made seems to be that children's 'literacy' is encapsulated within the English teacher's choice of set book! Beyond this, the questions are not even raised as to whether the 'types of reading' that are now possible in society might embrace non-print forms, or whether in certain definable respects pupils might prove to be more 'literate' than those who teach them.

Cultural and social assumptions relating to what we mean by 'literacy' are inescapable. Sarland calls 'literature' a 'highly problematic term', one he tends to avoid where possible. Our understanding of distinctions between terms such as 'literature' and 'literacy' are often hazy and unclear. I find it helpful to be reminded again by Margaret Meek (1991) of their provenance. Like her, I want to argue that we need to have a model of education which again brings the two words together:

> Until the middle of the eighteenth century literature and literacy meant almost the same thing. Literature was the books that a literate person read. Now we keep the words apart and give them specialized meanings; literacy for social usefulness, literature for certain selected texts that, by tradition or personal taste, are considered to be well-written and that are to be read, somehow, differently. I want to bring the two words together again so that literature does not depend for its definition on private opinions of its worth but is simply the writing that people do, while literacy is about reading and writing texts of all kinds and the entitlement of all. (p. 28)

We need to go beyond the National Curriculum for English if we are to find a rationale for the teaching of the subject which relates to contemporary society. In the context of multiliteracies, we need a curriculum which acknowledges that we can no longer escape from the fact that literature is only the writing that people do. Teaching literature, therefore, must involve consideration of a wide range of writing, and needs to move beyond traditionally known texts which are somehow 'handed down' from generation to generation in a way not available to other texts. If literacy is about reading and writing texts of all kinds, then it has to be seen as more than 'knowing the facts' of conventional orthography or of phonic systems. Literacy has to do with a quality of experience which the process of becoming increasingly literate enables and enriches; it has to do with cultivating the 'intelligence of feeling' which is an important part of being a more human individual. The process of becoming multiliterate will be a fundamental requirement for all young people in societies of the future; this is the challenge which our education systems cannot afford not to meet.

Redefining Literacy

Thus far, I am aware that what I have said is not new. I have been attempting to contextualize what I see as some important issues in our understanding of 'literature' and 'literacy'; in a very real sense I want to move beyond the connotations of these words to consider what it is about 'making meaning and value' that transcends them, and to begin to account for the fact that the making of meanings is of more fundamental importance than is some limited awareness of functional literacy in use, or even, for many, than a passing acquaintance with some old fictional texts.

To say that we need once again to redefine literacy is also to say nothing new. Recent historical periods (from the nineteenth century to the present) have seen definitions of the term amended at intervals, depending upon the specific nature of the policies being advocated at particular times. As recently as the mid-1980s Heath provided a review of then current definitions of literacy in the USA, commenting that 'current definitions of literacy held by policy-making groups are widely varied, and they differ markedly in the relationship they bear to the purposes and goals of reading and writing in the lives of individuals' (Heath, 1986a, p. 15). If we can all agree with Meek that 'literacy is not what it was' (Meek, 1991), we need to go on to acknowledge that it can never be so again. In preliterate Western society oral cultures transmitted knowledge and simultaneously enshrined value systems; the emergence of print no longer made that possible in the same way, since it served to disseminate thought and feeling on a wider cultural basis than the local and regional. The development of the major European languages, such as English, French and Portuguese, was economically driven in the age of Empires and had massive repercussions on our views of literacy as well as upon our idea of 'the literate person'. In recent history, literacy and economics have been intermeshed. In the present century, for example, we can trace an economic and political argument framing concepts of literacy in British government enquiries and reports, among them being 'Newbolt', 'Bullock' and 'Cox' (see, for example, Goodson and Medway, 1990; and Marum, 1995). One of the reasons why such policy reports have a limited (if historically interesting) impact on people's lives is that, in practice, they do not touch those lives at the level of daily living. Since different societies continue to accord different status to (in addition to retaining different definitions of) literacy, and since literacy continues to be perceived as having a range of social and individual uses related to differing lifestyles, policy documents by their nature are unable to encompass such a range of interpretation or to provide the basis for the coherent practical frameworks which need to be put in place to deliver massive literacy programmes. At one level, there is a continuing need to study further localized, small community uses of reading in order to discover distinctions in the uses of literacy. Heath's work in the Southeastern United States (1969–78), for example, is a clear indicator of the ways in which a community can view literacy for practical and social uses, and yet exclude from its priorities the more rarified school-based views of literacy it might and will encounter (Heath, 1986b).

At another level, as Campbell argues (chapter 6 in this volume), we need to retain a clear sense of the diminishing individuality of 'the local' in the face of the tremendous technological changes in communications which continue to accelerate as we approach the third millennium. Such developments offer two scenarios for the multiliterate society, and these continue to be debated, as this volume demonstrates. On the one hand Postman, cited by Simmons, warns of the danger of future cultures being seen as no more than 'a round of entertainments', part of society's trivial leisure pursuits. On the other, Campbell cites Greenhalgh when quoting students who say, 'We have developed ways of using it (technology) for our own ends. And the next generation will learn from us', in clear contradistinction from the 'dystopian doom and gloom' of academics.

Both these views, the optimistic and the pessimistic, arise from different cultural standpoints, as well as from different generations. This fact paradoxically helps to contextualize the subject of literacy, for it cannot after all be regarded from other than a sociohistorical context, as Graff has made clear in an illuminating article on the 'continuities and contradictions' surrounding the subject (Graff, 1986), and as Simmons has also so ably demonstrated from his own differing perspective (chapter 1 in this volume).

We need to be aware, therefore, that when we seek to redefine literacy in the contemporary setting we are prisoners of history, both of what has gone before us and of the societies we live in now, and that our notions of literacy are just as pragmatic and socially shaped as have been previous ones. To say this is not to offer a disclaimer; it is to contextualize ourselves and our societies in a longer-term cultural dimension which enables us to view literacy as a relative term and one which has tended in general to assume greater importance than it in fact may be argued to possess.

Barton (1994), for example, in a recent and valuable contribution to literacy studies, makes the following comment at an early stage of his developed argument:

> While there is undeniably a paradigm shift in the study of reading and writing, these changes are also part of more general trends in the social sciences towards being more reflexive, focusing on the particular, and of being interdisciplinary. Like other shifts, this one is also leading to conflicting ways of talking about the topic and to struggles over the meaning of words. (pp. 4–5)

In an historical sense, Barton's recent analysis follows in a developmental tradition established from the 1970s onwards, which has called for a redefinition of the subject in terms of contextually-defined literacies, while acknowledging the need to consider the continuities and contradictions inherent in the literacy debate. Graff (1986) acknowledges Olson (1975–6), for example, as among previous contributors to an intelligent widening of the debate on the significance of literacy:

> It (the significance of a universal high degree of literacy) is overvalued partly because literate people, such as educators, knowing the value of their own work, fail to recognize the value of anyone else's. More importantly, literacy is overvalued because of the very structure of formal schooling — schooling that, in Bruner's words, involves learning 'out of the context of action, by means that are primarily symbolic'. The currency of schools is words — words, as we saw earlier, that are shaped up for the requirements of literacy. We may have a distorted view of both the child and of social realities if we expect that the values and pleasures of literacy are so great that everyone, whether it is easy or difficult for him, or whether it leads to wealth or power . . . or not, is willing to invest the energy and time required to reach a high level of literacy. (quoted in Graff, 1986, p. 63)

Following on from Olson, writers such as Langer (1987) have argued the need for a more developed multiliterate approach to literacy studies, away from the narrow 'functional literacy' approaches of earlier writers, (as previously described by Simmons in this volume) pointing out previous mistakes at the level of policy and planning:

> . . . many scholars, as well as the general public, have regarded literacy somewhat narrowly — as the ability to read and write and get on at some minimal 'functional' level in day-to-day life and work — and . . . because of this restricted view, our solutions to very pragmatic issues of literacy learning and instruction have suffered, as have national interpretations of literacy-in-society for policy and planning.

The previous chapter of this volume has, I believe, clearly indicated that the 'literacy route' taken at policy level in the USA has been in many respects a prototype for that undertaken in the 1980s and 1990s by British policy-makers. Britain, however, has yet to acknowledge that it has taken a wrong turning in developing the National Curriculum proposals for English along the lines which have been followed over recent years. The USA has learned from its own mistakes; having come through a period of central directives, there is there now a dawning recognition of the need to embrace multiliterate approaches and to move to interdisciplinary approaches to literacy far more likely to prove productive in a pluralist, multiracial social context. Labov (1987) puts the position most succinctly:

> For many students who are aligned towards street culture and against classroom culture, certain of the sounds and words identified with classroom English are identified with a set of values that have already been rejected. They are associated with a set of polarities: white versus black, middle class versus working class, female versus male. They are associated with high culture versus popular culture in music, poetry, film and drama. They are associated with the school values of patterns of surveillance, submission to authority and informing on fellow students versus the street values of respect for privacy, resistance to oppression and loyalty to friends and equals. (pp. 144–5)

Until and unless policy-making in Britain takes account of the 'social realities' of British society, such government-directed steers as that underpinning the National Curriculum proposals will continue to meet powerful obstacles which will eventually defeat such narrowly-conceived policy. Among such obstacles, and not least in importance, will be the consciousnesses of teachers and pupils working together in schools. While literacy studies continues its 'struggle over the meaning of words' (Barton, 1994) teachers and pupils will go on with their daily lives. While the British Government believes that its latest educational idea (announced in the winter of 1995), the establishment of urban 'literacy centres', (viz. USA two decades ago) will add force to its educational programme, those working in state schools (pupils and teachers) continue to be underresourced and undervalued in a society which offers 'choice and diversity' only to those wealthy enough to benefit from such choice. The signs for the future are clear, unless policy direction is radically shifted to encompass a pluralistic, multiliteracies-based society of the third millennium.

Britain, in short, needs to go far beyond its present National Curriculum proposals to reconsider its future educational options. The 'new orders' for English, in particular, are woefully inadequate as a framework for the future advances in literacy which will be required in the fast-approaching future. The issue now is not what kind of society the present Government would like us to be: it is whether that society can continue in future to hold its Government in respect and for how long. Literacy has currency only in so far as it touches and shapes peoples' lives, and its potential for both good and evil is tremendous. Far from being a matter of 'knowing the facts', literacy is finally a means of establishing and acting upon identity; it needs, therefore, to be seen in its sociohistorical, living context:

Literacy in the abstract . . . can at most be viewed as a technique or set of techniques, a foundation in skills that can be developed, lost, or stagnated; at worst, literacy in the abstract is meaningless (Graff, 1986, p. 65).

References

BARTON, D. (1994) *Literacy: An Introduction to the Ecology of Written Language*, Oxford, Blackwell.

DES (1995) *English in the National Curriculum: Revised Orders*, London, HMSO, January.

FRY, D. (1985) *Children Talk about Books: Seeing Themselves as Readers*, Milton Keynes, Open University Press.

GOODSON, I. and MEDWAY, P. (1990) *Bringing English to Order*, London, Falmer Press.

GRAFF, H.J. (1986) 'The legacies of literacy: Continuities and contradictions in western society and culture' in DE CASTELL, S., LUKE, A. and EGAN, K (Eds) *Literacy, Society and Schooling: A Reader*, Cambridge, Cambridge University Press.

HEATH, S.B. (1986a) 'The functions and uses of literacy' in DE CASTELL, S., LUKE, A. and EGAN, K. (Eds) *Literacy, Society and Schooling: A Reader*, Cambridge, Cambridge University Press.

HEATH, S.B. (1986b) 'Critical factors in literacy development' in DE CASTELL, S., LUKE, A. and EGAN, K. (Eds) *Literacy, Society and Schooling: A Reader*, Cambridge, Cambridge University Press.

LABOV, W. (1987) 'The community as educator' in LANGER, J.A. (Ed.) *Language, Literacy and Culture: Issues of Society and Schooling*, Norwood, NJ, Ablex Publishing Corporation.

LANGER, J.A. (1987) 'A sociocognitive perspective on literacy' in LANGER, J.A. (Ed.) *Language, Literacy and Culture: Issues of Society and Schooling*, Norwood, NJ, Ablex Publishing Corporation.

MARUM, E. (Ed.) (1995) *Towards 2000: The Future of Childhood, Literacy and Schooling*, London, Falmer Press.

MEEK, M. (1991) *On Being Literate*, London, Bodley Head.

OLSON, D. (1975–76) quoted in Graff, H.J. (1986) p. 63.

SARLAND, C. (1991) *Young People Reading: Culture and Response*, Milton Keynes, Open University Press.

SCAA (1994) *The Review of the National Curriculum: A Report on the 1994 Consultation*, London, SCAA.

SCAA (1995) *One Week in March: A Survey of the Literature Pupils Read*, London, SCAA, December.

The National Curriculum for English — Some Useful References

BARRETT, P. (1992) 'The case for not revising the English order', *Language and Learning*, October.

BLACK, P. (1993) 'The shifting National Curriculum' in O'HEAR, P. and WHITE, J. (Eds) *Assessing the National Curriculum*, London, Paul Chapman Publishing.

CARTER, R. (1990) *Knowledge about Language and the Curriculum — The LINC Reader*, London, Hodder and Stoughton.

Cox, B. (1991) *Cox on Cox: An English Curriculum for the 1990s*, London, Hodder and Stoughton.

DFE (1995) *The Revised Orders for English in the National Curriculum*, London, HMSO.

Graham, D. (1993) *A Lesson for Us All: The Making of the National Curriculum*, London, Routledge.

Jones, K. (1992) *English and the National Curriculum: Cox's Revolution?*, London, Kogan Page.

Jones, K. (1994) in *English and Media Studies Magazine*, **30**, Summer.

NCC (1989a) *English for Ages 5–16* (The Cox Report), London, NCC.

NCC (1989b) *English for Ages 5–16* (the revised Pascall proposals), London, NCC.

NCC (1990) *English in the National Curriculum*, London, NCC.

Rosen, H. (1994) 'The whole story', *NATE News*, Summer.

Rosen, M. (1993) 'More heritages in England . . .' *NATE News*, Summer.

SCAA (1994) *English for Ages 5–16* (the Dearing Review), London, SCAA.

3   Core Curriculum; Cultural Heritage; Literacy: Recent Perspectives and Trends in Norwegian Education[1]

Bjørg B. Gundem

Introduction

In this chapter I discuss the place given to cultural heritage related to literacy in recent policy documents and in curriculum guidelines in Norway. The inherent arguments of the documents are linked to the necessity to secure the maintenance of a democratic society in providing personal development and extended literacy for all in a growing specialized and multicultural society. Inherent tensions and dilemmas are highlighted in the chapter, drawing attention to the fact that the main terms of reference for cultural heritage in the curriculum are Christian and Western humanistic values — it appears as though the schools are expected to inculcate a religious and humanistic-based monoculture at a time when the need to create scope for pluralism seems evident.

A rather extensive overview of the ongoing school reforms is given in order to provide a broad context for the issue as part of a redefinition of curriculum which highlights tradition as a vital element in the pursuit of a redefined curriculum. An analysis of why and how tradition came to be focussed on to a great degree is discussed, with reference to theory related to the arena of curriculum formulation.

Tradition is in my context understood as defined in a cultural, social or even political sense. And my topic is the specific ongoing development of curriculum taking place in my country and the role of tradition as part of this development at the national-political level. My sources for identifying and analyzing this process are, in particular, three policy texts from the Royal Ministry of Education, Research and Church Affairs: *Education in Norway, Core Curriculum for Primary, Secondary and Adult Education,* and *Principles and Guidelines for the Structure, Organization and Content of the 10-year Compulsory School,* all dating from the period 1993–94.[2]

The chapter has four parts. In the first I give an overview of the present school reform in Norway, emphasizing the curriculum reform in basic schooling.

The second part concerns what may be called the context of influence and the context of policy text production as a precondition for a redefinition of curriculum documents in terms of tradition (Ball, 1990; Bowe and Ball, 1992).

The third section describes aspects of the substantive areas implied and the rhetoric or arguments involved, and adds some comments as to my understanding of embedded promises and paradoxes.

In the fourth part certain aspects that I see as especially problematic, but also hopeful indicators, are discussed.

Some Remarks

It may be a matter of critique that my description is largely based on politically-stated determining and influencing forces, and that I do not pay equal attention to underlying economic and ideological structures and power relations. From an inside perspective, national curriculum-making is probably a practical problem solving enterprise. To what degree curriculum proposals come about as compromises reached through substantive and ideological discussions is unclear. More probably they arise mainly from an interaction between policy decisions, framework factors, incidental events and practical considerations (cp. Carlgren, 1995).

Further, I run the danger of conveying a sort of skewed picture, as the point of focus will be the question of tradition in the curriculum — leaving other important aspects aside.

There is in my presentation no discussion of the term literacy and the concept is more implicitly than explicitly treated.

School Reform as Curriculum Reform

A Curriculum-driven Systemic Reform

It is possible to view the curriculum reform going on in many countries today as part of a universal movement towards restructuring the educational systems of Western welfare states. One may say that the term 'reconstructing' denotes in certain countries the establishment of the educational market as well as a change in governing and decentralization-centralization measures (*ibid.*). As to centralization, decentralization and steering strategies, a marked international harmonization is taking place. Countries which used to be highly centralized in their curriculum work, like Norway and Sweden, have, during the last decade, experienced school-based curriculum work and countries like England which were locally oriented in curricular terms have got a national curriculum (cp. Skilbeck, 1990). Steering strategies such as governing by objectives and increased attention to assessment and evaluation may, however, be said to be leading to a curriculum reality where curricular decentralization through governing and evaluation strategies in practice takes the form of curricular centralization (cp. Gundem, 1993b). On the one hand the Norwegian curriculum reform may be treated as a case study within this reconstructional context. On the other, it entails elements and considerations that go far beyond narrow reconstructional concerns and strategies, implying existential and human considerations for the future of the individual person and for democracy, and for future generations as well. While the question of cultural literacy may be linked to concerns for the individual person and for the maintenance of democracy, problems linked to environmental or ecological literacy seem related to the second factor.

One way to put it, is to say that the school reforms taking place in Norway at the moment may be characterized as being a 'systemic reform' and in fact are a curriculum-driven systemic reform. What is meant by systemic reform may differ from country to country.[3] In a Norwegian setting it makes sense to characterize systemic reform in the curriculum field as a reform that is: (i) part of a wider reform of the educational and societal system; (ii) part of a comprehensive educational reform aimed at all levels of education; (iii) a reform implying coherence among school types within the school system; (iv) a reform striving for goal coherence: that is national overarching goals translated into goals for all school subjects and into curriculum programs at school levels; and (v) a reform being translated into implementation through taking into consideration, in the planning of strategies, all relevant factors and constraints — including teacher education and assessment.

In relation to these points, I will just make a few remarks.

(i) The curriculum reform is in fact part of a wider educational and societal reform implying:

— a school reform where all children are accepted for the compulsory school at the age of 6, and compulsory education is extended to 10 years;

— a childrens' reform which makes the school responsible for helping to provide a good environment for children to grow up in, emphasizing rich impulses and extensive opportunities for learning, play and their own chosen activities, and also gives room for varied activities together with adults in different roles;

— a family reform, which places the emphasis on cooperation between home, school and the local community, and a further development of day-centre arrangements which meet children's need for a secure and pleasant place to be while their parents are at work;

— a cultural reform, where activities in the local community, ranging for example from the arts to the more practical crafts, are strengthened and further developed in cooperation with the school, the day-care centre system and the municipal music schools (Min. Ed. Doc, 1994c, p. 1).

In relation to the last point about cultural reform (especially aesthetic and artistic literacy as an entitlement for everyone), this has resulted in completely (even dramatically) new curriculum guidelines for its implementation (KUF, 20 July 1995, pp. 1–17).

(ii) As to the point about systemic reform as part of a comprehensive educational reform aimed at all levels of education from preschool education to university education, it may be said that reform along these lines is actually taking place (cp. Min. Ed. Doc, 1990; KUF, 1994a and 1994b). The reform of teacher education was, for example, opened by a large conference this November. According to public and academic debate the speed and extensiveness of this comprehensive reform is, to put it mildly, a matter of controversy.

(iii) Perhaps the most obvious and marked characteristic of the reform is that it implies coherence amongst school types within the school system. The means to accomplish this is first and foremost a common core curriculum, or a type of nationally mandated curriculum guideline which is in fact a general policy curriculum document for primary, secondary and adult education alike — called a core curriculum. 'Core' is here used in a special way — denoting underlying principles and aims meant to be common to all schools as defined by central bodies, and not a common core of factual knowledge and skills to be mastered by everyone. In many ways this new core curriculum is at the heart of the reform — it is, to put it differently, the 'raison d'être' of the reform. For a policy document to attain this role and address itself not only to teachers and pupils, but to parents and the general public as well, rather drastic demands relating to form and content may have seemed pertinent.

From the 1960s until last year, the different curriculum guidelines produced have had the same format and type of structure and language. A completely new layout, extensive use of pictures, less expert language and even a return to old fashioned expressions denoting virtues like 'diligence', have made critical voices say that the most recent reform is a complete break with the traditions of curriculum guidelines in our country.

The changes are, however, also of a different kind. There is an explicit endeavour to link the essence and spirit of different Education Acts, and of recent white papers related to educational matters, directly to the core curriculum, at the same time safeguarding the embedded messages of former curriculum guidelines. This has resulted on the one hand in a presentation of overarching principles as well as of aims defined as (a) something to work towards and as (b) something one knows whether one analyzes them closely or not. On the other hand, the changes have resulted in the presentation of the contents of the core curriculum under the following headings: the spiritual human being; the creative human being;

the working human being; the liberally-educated human being; the social human being; the environmentally-aware human being; and the integrated human being.

(iv) As to the point about a reform striving for goal coherence — that is to make sure that national overarching goals are translated into goals for all school subjects and into curriculum programs at school levels, a great effort is being made to make sure that this is happening. The curriculum guideline or syllabus for every school subject should be in accordance with the overarching principles and aims laid down in the core curriculum in terms of its rhetoric; it should also demonstrate that such principles are also an integrated and integrating element of the subject syllabus. To give an example: all school subjects have aesthetic and ethical dimensions which should be revealed and highlighted in the curriculum.

(v) Perhaps the most difficult questions are linked to the process of implementation. I shall highlight certain aspects, being unable in this context to sketch out the full picture.

In many ways implementation is linked to decentralization strategies, based upon the realization of previous failures to implement top to bottom reforms. My first point relates to changes due to decentralization processes implying local or school-based curriculum development. Until the mid-1980s, school-based curriculum development was non-existent except for a few research projects during the 1970s, such as the famous 'Lofot-project'. The curriculum guidelines of 1985 and 1987 mandated, however, local curriculum work both from the point of view of locally-orientated contents and local adaptations of national prescribed syllabi. It is important to notice that to start with it was a pedagogical strategy embodying all the virtues in Norwegian schooling such as school self-renewal, teacher professionalization, pupil-adapted curricula, parents' involvement and school democratization. A new decentralized income allocation system due to new municipal legislation in 1986 has, however, added an administrative-political aspect, implying tensions and constraints of economic and political kinds and linked to the relation between the professionals (the teachers) and local political and administrative authorities (cp. Gundem, 1993a and 1993b). In spite of these tensions school-based curriculum work is at the heart of the implementation project for the present curriculum reform, stressing another highlighted aspect of the new approach. This is my second point: there is a demand for and an expectancy of an increased sense of 'responsibility'. Needless to say, the devolution of responsibility attached to the different levels of curriculum decision-making is accentuated and, in fact, dramatic.

Another aspect in regard to implementation is linked to the fact that the latest national core curriculum addresses all of primary, secondary and adult education. An additional underlying motive for such a common general core curriculum is an effort to make the school system as a whole more effective and flexible in relation to international and national demands and tendencies. The existing institutionalized separation between different school levels within the national school system is regarded as detrimental in terms of change and reform. There will, of course, be additional guidelines produced, aimed at the specific school levels. But the fact that a common general curriculum guideline has been established implies what we may characterize as a turning away from the differentiating process of compartmentalization (Gundem, 1993; Haft and Hopmann, 1990).

Summary

In summary, it may be possible to say that the present curriculum reform in Norway is driven by a strategic priority placed on pedagogical processes in order to support empowerment of the individual. The primary reform values are linked to personal autonomy, participation and democracy. It is in this context that I shall look at cultural literacy — using the term 'cultural' first and foremost in its ascribed meaning relating to traditional culture.

But first, some remarks about why and how tradition came to be focused in such a conspicuous way.

The Context of Influence and the Context of Policy Text Formulation

The stated justifications at the educational-political level for a new core curriculum for primary, secondary and adult education are linked to changes in society and to changes in the school system. It is the changes in society that are especially of interest in this connection.[4]

These changes are stated as changes concerning:

— the family situation — including the personal aspect;
— internationalization — including an economic aspect;
— mass media explosion — the question of values and norms;
— multiculturalism — the question of cultural diversity and language minorities.

There is nothing new or unique in this. It is on the contrary very similar to what has been put forth in recent documents from the Organization for Economic Cooperation and Development/Centre for Educational Research and Innovation (OECD/CERI) as common to the OECD countries (Skilbeck, 1990; OECD/CERI, 1994). A closer look into the policy documents reveals a particularly high degree of concern relating to purposes and priorities concerning what sort of people are needed in our world today, in terms of these issues, and a resulting concern that the curriculum should contribute towards fostering such developments.[5] It is on this subject that the cultural, social and political traditions enter the reforms in a very conspicuous way, as a means towards attainment of educational aims and goals in a value perspective.[6]

In order, however, to explain how it was possible for this to happen, it will be useful to look closer at the context that constituted the arena of formulation (Lindensjö and Lundgren, 1986) or, in other words, the context of policy text production. This relates to major changes having taken place in curriculum work at the national level. Most remarkable is the replacement of a traditional curriculum committee by three reference groups, consulting bodies or 'working parties', and with the Minister of Education as the chief entrepreneur and author, assisted by his staff. One of the reference groups, in particular, consisted of members representing different spheres of intellectual life and interest groups, and was in fact influential in producing and formulating the first policy document on the school-society relationship, a document strong in restorative thinking. Educational experts were altogether scarce in these groups — only one in each group and each one not particularly representative of the 'new progressives'.[7] Representatives from the teacher unions were altogether wanting. In summary, an analysis of the context of policy text production makes evident a marked shift in what has been called the triangle of tension regarding influencing forces on school politics (Ball, 1990). The professional elements are squeezed out, leaving some room for certain societal interest groups, while the dominant deciding forces are political in nature.

Cultural Tradition as a Means Embedded in the Curriculum — Curriculum as Intentional Political Action

An understanding of the context of policy text production and formulation seems important in terms of the role given to tradition in relation to values particularly connected to four domains: the personal, societal-democratic, international, and multicultural, and also to sources of knowledge for example, traditions of knowledge production. In the following description of these I switch to a certain degree from an outsider perspective to an insider one — using the words and formulations of the involved parties — presenting curriculum texts as intentional political action.

Personal Development, Democracy and Cultural Heritage

In relation to the personal development of the individual citizen the cultural heritage is considered as an important source in two respects particularly. On the one hand it is argued that the development of individual identity occurs through becoming familiar with inherited forms of conduct, norms of behaviour and modes of expression. The curriculum should consequently elaborate and deepen the learner's familiarity with national and local traditions. The bonds between generations will become closer when they share experiences and insights, stories, songs and legends.

On the other hand, the curriculum must play a leading role in passing on the common heritage, the culture with which all must be familiar if society is to remain democratic. The link between the maintenance of democracy, cultural heritage and a common knowledge base is further elaborated by stressing a common national subject matter. There is a strong political will to extend and gradually widen the common national subject matter as the pupils move upwards through the different grades in school and this common national syllabus is meant to be clearly specified for the different subjects (KUF, 1994c). This may seem a paradox concerning the democratic development of school and society, because it clearly diminishes the role of the teachers and the students in deciding what to teach and learn. The main arguments advanced, however, are related to the question of equity and equal rights and to a more subtle line of thinking: In an increasingly specialized society a common frame of reference must be the property of all people, in order to escape differences in competence which may otherwise surface into social inequality and be what is termed 'abused by undemocratic forces'. This last hint in my view relates the recent reforms to political and religious, as well as to ideological, fundamentalism.

It is argued that those who do not share a knowledge of the background information taken for granted in public discourse will often overlook the points in question and miss the meaning. It is underscored that newcomers to the country are more easily incorporated into our society when implicit features of our cultural heritage are made clear and exposed to view, and that knowledge about past events and achievements unites people over time.

Examples given of common contexts as references for understanding encompass, for example, historical events, constitutional principles, the classics of literature and the symbols used on weather charts. Without this overarching comprehension, it is argued, it will be difficult for non-specialists to participate in decisions that affect their lives, underlining the fact that the more specialized and technological our culture becomes, the more difficult it will be to communicate across professional boundaries (KUF, 1994a, pp. 26–7).[8]

So far the picture looks bright and promising. The way it is interpreted, misinterpreted, discussed and attacked in academic and public debate, however, provides a darker picture: a fear of a return to basics and to theory at the expense of the weakest and less gifted pupils.

Multiculturalism and the Appreciation of Tradition

The tensions and dilemmas are even more evident in relation to multiculturalism. On the one hand, it is maintained that our domestic history and distinctive features are our contribution to the cultural diversity of the world. Our cultural heritage must therefore be central as an integral part of the mandated curriculum. On the other hand, there is a general understanding that the ethnic and cultural diversity of today's society must be visible in the curriculum. The national curriculum documents provide curriculum guidelines as steering documents for the teaching of language minorities and multicultural education, as well as safeguarding cultural diversity by mandating aspects of different ethnic cultures to be made visible across different school subjects and themes. The Sami language and culture are, for example, part of the common heritage which Norway has a special responsibility to safeguard. Aspects of Sami traditional culture should consequently be introduced into school subjects like music (the 'joik'), sports (throwing the 'lasso'), and natural science (for example, the balance of the ecosystem related to reindeer keeping).

In addition the school system embraces many pupils from groups which in our country constitute minority cultures and languages. The curriculum must therefore, according to stated political intentions, convey knowledge of other cultures and take advantage of the potential for enrichment that the interaction of minority groups and Norwegians with another cultural heritage represents.

I see a paradox relating to statements such as this, for the main terms of reference for cultural heritage in the curriculum are Christian and Western humanistic values — and it may well seem that schools are expected to inculcate a religious and humanistic-based monoculture at a time when the need to create scope for pluralism seems evident (cp. Englund, 1994). It is symptomatic that the draft proposal for the curriculum guidelines for religious instruction, focussing mainly on Christianity, but including other religions and beliefs as well, will be compulsory for all pupils and also encompass the former separate instruction which was offered under the heading of morals and ethics (KUF, 20 July 1995, pp. 1–16). The main argument advanced is the need for a common religious 'literacy' for all Norwegian people, notwithstanding ethnic, religious and cultural backgrounds. This has, of course, resulted in a storm of debate and protest, especially on the part of Muslims, Jews and agnostics — who have literally joined forces in together forming a protest organization. Adding to the heated discussion is the fact that an application for state grant support for a Muslim school under the Norwegian Education Act has been repeatedly rejected by the Ministry of Education, Research and Church Affairs. Among the loud voices of critique I select Lars Løvlie, an Oslo University professor:

> We are used to thinking of the past 250 years — what we call modernity — in terms of Enlightenment rationality, more specifically as the proud realization of a scientific spirit which shattered superstition and prejudice, of a humanity which tolerated differences in race, religion and ethnic background, and of an idea of justice which makes all individuals equal under the law. The most obvious paradox is of course that the explicit reaffirmation of the European tradition and of national culture under the present political conditions proceeds by an actual

emptying of such terms as freedom, responsibility and solidarity . . . The humanistic, universalistic and liberal tradition of modernity is now replaced by ethnocentricism, difference and particularity. (Løvlie, 1995, pp. 3–4)

And further: a main impression derived from the curriculum texts is that the ideal expectation is that the non-Norwegian speaking pupil 'grows into' the Norwegian society in every sense.

Internationalization and the Appreciation of Tradition

The importance of the cultural heritage is also of relevance in the context of handling the flow of internationalization. It is maintained that growing world-wide internationalization and influences from the global community demand a heightened awareness of one's own tradition and values, and that the increasing specialization and complexity of the global community requires a deepened familiarity with the main currents and traditional elements of the national culture. The expansion of knowledge demands heightened awareness of the values that must guide the choices of the individual person. A main point I wish to emphasize is that, when transitions are massive and changes rapid, it becomes even more pressing to emphasize historical orientation, national distinctiveness and local variation in order to safeguard our identity. It is also relevant to point out that our contribution to the global community relates to tradition in specific ways (KUF, 1994a, pp. 28–9).

It is in my view a paradox that internationalization is seen to such a great extent in relation to tradition and not in the context of a future vision, or at least a future perspective, and that the answer to our existential, societal and global problems is claimed to lie to such a large degree in the virtues of the past and in our national heritage.

I recently read a report dealing with the lack of global perspectives, relating especially to the 'third world', in the 1994 syllabus for the upper secondary school. It is argued that this may have developed from the new general core curriculum, where concepts such as our inherited common culture and traditions are repeatedly mentioned, without drawing a connecting line to other countries and cultures and without revealing the negative side of such a position. The report concludes that the result is a chauvinistic world view (Nordkvelle, 1993).

Knowledge Traditions

Of interest in relation to the question of literacy and to 'what knowledge is of most worth' is the view presented in the core curriculum. In relation to a knowledge base for choosing the content of schooling, the curriculum, three different traditions are recognized and in principle they are given equal status. It is explicitly stated that the curriculum must build upon and demonstrate the contributions of the past concerning (i) innovative work; (ii) intellectual inquiry; and (iii) artistic expression (KUF, 1994a, pp. 12–13). The promise of future advancement is linked to familiarity with the past in all three domains.

(i)   The first tradition is characterized as experienced-based knowledge — derived from practical work and learning through experience. In particular, the aspect of improvement by trial and error is heavily emphasized and countless examples provided to underscore the point. In this context the concept of tacit knowledge, lodged in the hands and mediated by use, is brought to the forefront.

(ii)   The second tradition relates to school subjects where new knowledge is won through theoretical development, tested by logic and facts, experience, evidence and research.

(iii) The third tradition is the cultural tradition, defined in such formulations as 'by body and mind and embedded in arts and crafts, in language and literature, in theatre, song, music, dance and athletics' (*ibid.*, p. 13).

What is interesting is that the three modes of knowledge are all treated as traditions and that the promise of future development and improvement is linked to familiarity not only with the manifest results of the past but with the continuous development and antecedents of today's status quo.[9] It is a positive feature that it is stressed that in many trades and professions all three traditions interlace. It is, however, not so positive a fact that the tendency towards more emphasis on traditional school subjects linked to academic disciplines works counter to these underlying principles. In the ongoing curriculum development work, insufficient attention has been given to all three aspects of knowledge.[10]

Another paradox may be linked to the importance attached to pupils learning not to perceive science and its theories as eternal and absolute truths. Consequently the curriculum must seek that difficult balance between respect for established knowledge and the critical attitude that is necessary for developing new learning and for organizing information in new ways. Education must instill an awareness of the limitations of the current body of knowledge, as well as the realization that predominant doctrines can block fresh insights.

Another paradox is linked to the understanding of our technological heritage. Familiarity with our technological heritage — the easing of life and the improvement technological development has furnished, but also the dangers technological inventions have introduced — must be an essential element of the curriculum. Perhaps two aspects are of most importance — the relationship between natural science, ecology and ethics and the interplay between economy, ecology and technology. These are important aspects of what may be called scientific, technological and ecological literacies. The paradox and promise of tradition are particularly embedded in the conflicts of interests inherent in these relations.

Discussion

Amelioration of Society through Schooling

My first comments are linked to the strong emphasis laid in the curricular documentation on both the role of schooling and the curriculum, in terms of the amelioration of society through empowering the individual. In my country we have an expression denoting schooling as anti-current culture, of current culture as denoting decay — and it is a tradition to look upon the role of schooling as important in this respect.

Do we see hope — does a curriculum policy document like this one convey promise, or is it a paradox to expect that schooling may yield more productively than the society of which it is part? I see, however, a challenge arising from this situation — it is a challenge to find new strategies in our curriculum thinking, new modes of thought and action.[11] It is in fact a paradox that a document like this amounts to no more than an array of slogans, which will acquire real meaning only if it is put into practical action.

The Problematics of Value Teaching

The American curriculum professor Arthur Foshay wrote, after he had read the English version of the core-curriculum, that he envied us the possibility of including matters of a spiritual, moral, creative, cooperative and ecological nature, and he was curious how this curriculum guideline would be put into practice. He also sent me an article: 'Values as object matter: The reluctant pursuit of heaven'. His letter and his article made me think and realize that what this debate is all about is the teaching of values — it is in fact an effort to teach values directly. Recently I had to write a comment to the second draft of the different subjects' syllabi for our basic ten-year school, and found an occasion to underline the importance of stressing verbs used in connection with values as aims — indicating ways of teaching values suggested by Foshay.[12]

The Symbolic Power of Linking the Past and the National

I find the overwhelming emphasis placed on the national heritage rather disturbing. The symbolic power of linking values to the past and to the national is, however, significant, and it has been exploited dramaturgically and rhetorically — also in actions such as those of the Minister of Education, who launched the core-curriculum sitting on an old school desk and made the audience sing a well-known and rather sentimental folksong (Reite, 1995).

The Rhetorics of Curriculum Reform

What I also see as an overarching paradox is the persistent belief on the part of the curriculum authorities, and also in public debate on the role and place of curriculum documents, that they can initiate and implement a curriculum reform that will make people different and the world a better place to be. At the same time there are, however, clear signals on the national and local arena that there is a growing awareness of the complexities and problems relating to the implementation and realization of curriculum reform.

One is the pronounced statement that the curriculum guidelines (and not textbooks or tests) shall decide what knowledge is of most worth — realizing however the enormous influence that textbooks in particular have had in the past. Another is the seriousness and insistence upon moral and ethical responsibility on national, regional and local levels related not only to national welfare but to the existential and global crises of today.

A third sign is the turning to curriculum theory in order to find help in making sense of the events and confusion of curriculum practice.

Conclusion

Critical analysis of national curriculum policies, including critical scrutiny of policy texts, is one of the tasks of the curriculum researcher. Another is the provision of constructive contributions to strategies for identifying curriculum problems and for alternative strategies and solutions to these problems. A promise and a paradox in the present Norwegian situation is the turning to curriculum theory on the part of national, regional and local school authorities as a means of elucidating the situation and finding alternative answers to curriculum problems. The lack of implementation of state mandated curriculum reform has, apart from legitimating local curriculum work, led to a search for theories illuminating the nature of curriculum problems. The thinking of Joseph J. Schwab, for example in his essays on 'The practical', has proved influential as part of research studies and as an approach to curriculum work in different contexts, both in and out of school settings.

Another example is related to William A. Reid's thinking concerning different yet competing curriculum interests and the resolution of problems through curriculum deliberation in the common public interest (Reid, 1992 and 1994). In presenting these thoughts to curriculum committees at national level, to administrators and teachers at regional and local levels, and also to curriculum students and professors in colleges and universities, I find a growing understanding of the complexities, and paradoxes, but also of the promises and possibilities related to the curriculum field. Reid once stressed that we need to realize the incremental nature of curriculum change. 'There will be change, but in an incremental way'. But this change is, and will be, dependent on the teachers' involvement in and responsibility for that change. A Swedish educational researcher, Ingrid Carlgren (1995) argues that the link to teacher professionalism in today's curriculum situation will be that teachers and other people at grass roots level will have theoretical concepts and categories to describe and name their own curriculum situation — a teachers'/practitioners' curriculum literacy.

Among the important issues concerning the curriculum for the twenty-first century are the impending questions concerning lifelong learning and literacy. In many ways they are interwined. There will be no lifelong learning for the individual person without literate capacities being demonstrated in a wide range of fields. It is, however, estimated that one-third of all adults in most OECD countries have attained only basic standards of literacy. That constitutes major challenges for educational systems in most countries — challenges that must be seen against a background of growing unemployment, and deep concerns over future job prospects, with marginalization and social exclusion as a reality for many people. The question of literacy must be seen in this context — not only as a political or ideological problem, but as a practical one that needs alternative practical solutions based on deliberation, prudence and negotiation (Schwab 1978).

Notes

1   An earlier version of this article was presented at the annual meeting of the American Educational Research Association, April 1995.
2   I refer to versions translated into English: *Core Curriculum for Primary, Secondary and Adult Education* (1994), *Education in Norway* (May 1994) and *Principles and Guidelines for the Structure, Organization and Content of the 10-year Compulsory School* (draft version 1994). The last one is an English translation of main points in Report to the Parliament (St. Meld) no 29 (1994–1995).
3   At the meeting of OECD/CERI held at Fort Myers, USA, 1995 the distinction made was between three types of systemic reform: 'teacher initiated', 'standards driven' and 'curriculum driven' reform.
4   The stated reasons for curriculum change relating to changes in the school system are:

> — introduction of a program for after school activities;
> — lowering the school starting age to six years;
> — a three year upper secondary compulsory education for all;
> — the efforts towards a pedagogically more flexible school system (making more effective teaching and learning possible in view of rapidly changing national and international conditions related to what is important to teach and learn) — 'What knowledge is of most worth'.

5   For example, what kind of people do we want:

> The aim of education is to furnish children, young people and adults with the tools they need to face the tasks of life and its challenges together with others — to provide learners with the capability to take charge

of themselves and their lives — qualify for productive participation in today's labour force, supply a basis for later shifts to not envisaged occupations — develop skills needed for specialized tasks and provide a general level of competence — train young people to make sound choices and to take responsibility, and to assess the effects of their actions on others and evaluate them in terms of ethical principles.

> The aim of education is to expand the individual's capacity to perceive and to participate, to experience, to empathize and to excel. (KUF, 1994a, p. 5)

In the case of internationalization:

> — to combine technical know-how with human insight;
> — to develop a workforce that is highly qualified and versatile;
> — to combine an international outlook with a deepened familiarity of national traditions;
> — to make it possible for Norway to exert international influence in especially two domains: developing the common welfare of the world, and protection of the environment of the world. (*ibid.*, pp. 28–9)

And in relation to multiculturalism: There is a broad understanding that the ethnic and cultural diversity of today's society must be visible in the curriculum. The national curriculum documents provide curriculum guidelines as steering documents for the teaching of language minorities and multicultural education, as well as safeguarding cultural diversity by mandating aspects of different ethnic cultures to be made visible across different school subjects and themes.

6 I will just quote regarding values and norms:

> Education in Norway is based on fundamental Christian and humanistic values demanding and fostering tolerance, equality, human rights and rationality, emphasizing charity, brotherhood and hope.
>   Children and adolescents must be made to understand moral claims and the canons that are valid in society and allow them to inform their conduct.
>   Education must clarify and justify ethical principles and norms. Pupils must be confronted with choices that are tested against the norms on which the school and society as a whole are built. And educators as role models should lead the way by their example. There should be close interaction between upbringing at home and the education provided by the school. (KUF, 1994a, pp. 7–8)

7 I was myself the only 'curriculum professor' in one of the reference groups.
8 Expressed in terms of policy:

> Common background knowledge is thus at the core of a national network of communications between members of a democratic society. It is the common frames of reference which make it possible to link what one sees and reads to a shared tacit mode of thinking. It makes it possible to fathom complex messages and to interpret new ideas, situations and challenges. (KUF, 1994a, pp. 26–7)

9 To give a quotation:

> Common to all three traditions is that they fuse the human gifts of cre-
> ating and experiencing. They show how pursuits in different areas have
> produced works of lasting value. They highlight the rich heritage from
> the past in our custody and they display mankind's scope for continuing
> progress. (p. 14)

10 My comment is based on studying the draft proposal for the syllabi of the different subjects.
11 For example, the curriculum matrix presented by William Doll in his book *A post-Modern Perspective on Curriculum* (New York, Teachers College, Columbia University Press). See also Reid (1992) and (1994).
12 Foshay specifically suggests four modes of teaching: by accretion, by traumatic experience, by association and by teaching vicariously (Foshay 1993, pp. 50–1).

References

BALL, S.J. (1990) *Politics and Policy Making in Education: Explorations in Policy Sociology*, London, Routledge.

BOWE, R. and BALL, S.J. with GOLD, A. (1992) *Reforming Education and Changing Schools: Case Studies in Policy Sociology*, London: Routledge.

CARLGREN, I. (1995) 'National curriculum as social compromise or discursive politics? Some reflections on a curriculum-making process', *Journal of Curriculum Studies*, 27, 4.

ENGLUND, T. (1994) 'New international trends for Swedish schools — Marketization, privatization, religiousization, languagezation . . .' in KALLOS, D. and LINDBLAD, S. (Eds) *New Policy Contexts for Education: Sweden and United Kingdom*, Umeå, Pedagogiska institutionen, Umeå Universitet, pp. 66–100.

FOSHEY, A.W. (1993) 'Values as object matter: The reluctant pursuit of heaven', *Journal of Curriculum and Supervision*, Fall, 9, 1, pp. 41–52.

GUNDEM, B.B. (1993a) *Mot en ny skolevirkelighet: Læreplanene i et sentraliserings-desentraliseringsperspektiv*, (Towards a New Reality of Schooling: Curriculum and the Local–National Dilemma) Oslo, Ad Notam Gyldendal.

GUNDEM, B.B. (1993b) 'Rise, development and changing conceptions of curriculum administration and curriculum guidelines in Norway: The national–local dilemma', *Journal of Curriculum Studies*, 25, 3.

GUNDEM, B.B. (1995) 'Redefining the curriculum: The place and role of tradition: The case of the Norwegian "core" curriculum', paper presented at the annual meeting of the American Educational Research Association, April, San Francisco.

HAFT, H. and HOPMANN, S. (1990) 'History: Curriculum making as symbolic action' in HAFT, H. and HENNING, S. (Eds) *Case Studies in Curriculum Administration History*, London, Falmer Press, pp. 159–73.

KIRKE, UTDANNINGS- OG FORSKNINGSDEPARTEMENTET, ST. MELD NR 29 (1994–1995) Om prinsipper og retningslinjer for 10-årig grunnskole — ny læreplan.

KIRKE, UTDANNINGS- OG FORSKNINGSDEPARTEMENTET, KUF (20 July 1995) *Læreplan for fag i 10-årig grunnskole, L97, Høringsutkast* (Curriculum Guideline for School Subjects in the Basic 10 Year School).

NATIONAL PARENTS' COMMITTEE FOR PRIMARY AND LOWER SECONDARY EDUCATION (FUG) (nd) *Information about the National Parents' Committee for Primary and Lower Secondary Education.*

NORDKVELLE, Y. (1993) 'Internasjonalisering i skolen, Hva bringer de nye læreplanene?' (Internationalization in Schools: What do the syllabi provide?), Lillehammer, Oppland Regional College.

LINDENSJÖ, B. and LUNDGREN, U.P. (1986) *Politisk styrning och utbildningsreformer* (Political Governing and Educational Reforms), Stockholm, Liber.

LØVLIE, L. (1995) 'Paradoxes of curriculum reform', paper presented at the conference 'Didaktik and/or Curriculum: A Continuing International Dialogue', August, Universitet i Oslo.

ORGANIZATION FOR ECONOMIC COOPERATION AND DEVELOPMENT/CENTRE FOR EDUCATIONAL RESEARCH AND INNOVATION (1994) *The Curriculum Redefined: Schooling for the 21st Century*, Paris, OECD/CERI.

REID, W.A. (1978) *Thinking about the Curriculum: The Nature of and Treatment of Curriculum Problems*, London, Routledge and Kegan Paul.

REID, W.A. (1992) *The Pursuit of Curriculum: Schooling and the Public Interest*, Norwood, NJ, Ablex Publishing Corporation.

REID, W.A. (1994) *Curriculum Planning as Deliberation*, Report no. 11, University of Oslo, Institute for Educational Research.

REITE, E.J. (1995) *Statlig læreplanadministrering: Styring. strategi — Retorikk* (National curriculum administration: Governance – strategies – rhetorics), University of Oslo, Institute for Educational Research.

ROYAL MINISTRY OF EDUCATION, RESEARCH AND CHURCH AFFAIRS: REPORT NO. 37 TO THE STORTING (1990–1991) Concerning organization and management in the education sector. Summary.

ROYAL MINISTRY OF EDUCATION, RESEARCH AND CHURCH AFFAIRS, KUF (1974a) *Core Curriculum for Primary, Secondary and Adult Education*, Oslo, KUF.

ROYAL MINISTRY OF EDUCATION, RESEARCH AND CHURCH AFFAIRS, KUF (1994b) *Education in Norway*, Oslo, KUF.

ROYAL MINISTRY OF EDUCATION, RESEARCH AND CHURCH AFFAIRS, KUF (1994c) *Principles and Guidelines for the Structure, Organization and Content of the 10-year Compulsory School*, draft version, Oslo, KUF.

SCHWAB, J.J. (1978) 'The practical: A language for curriculum'; 'The practical: Arts of eclectic'; 'The practical: Translation into curriculum' in WESTBURY, I. and WILKOF, N.J. (Eds) *Science, Curriculum and Liberal Education: Selected Essays of Joseph J. Schwab*, Chicago, IL, University of Chicago Press, pp. 278–383.

SKILBECK, M. (1990) *Curriculum Reform — An Overview of Trends*, Paris, OECD/CERI.

Section 2

Teaching and Research Perspectives on Literacy

4 How Do We Evaluate the Literature Curriculum?: About a Social Frame of Reference

Gert Rijlaarsdam and Tanja Janssen

Literature Teaching in the Netherlands

As a general rule, Dutch children receive no teaching of literature until the fourth year of secondary school. The main emphasis on literature teaching comes in the fifth and sixth years, when the students are 16–18-years-old. Of course, there is a lot of reading of fiction and non-fiction in lower secondary education, but only in higher secondary education has the teaching of literature a formal status. Educational policy is changing now towards a more centralized curriculum, but in Dutch culture this kind of centralization is as nothing compared to the UK, for instance. Freedom and autonomy are features in the field of education that prevent the Dutch government from centralizing to the degree found in such countries as England and Greece. Although we have central exams for secondary education, teachers have a lot of freedom with regard to aims and methods of teaching, especially in the Mother tongue curriculum, which in the Netherlands includes Dutch language and literature. Even now, when a need is felt among teachers to formulate aims more centrally in order to avoid possible curricular chaos, centralization will not affect the 'standard' differences in teaching. In order to contextualize the procedures we will provide for the evaluation of the literature curriculum, we will first provide some information about the literature curriculum in the Netherlands. Although we have stressed the differences existing in aims and methods, we will now give some general facts, extracted from a national survey we carried out (Janssen and Rijlaarsdam, 1992a; Janssen and Rijlaarsdam, 1995).

In the Netherlands, teachers spend about three hours a week on teaching a class in Dutch language and literature in higher secondary education. The workload of teachers is about twenty-nine hours teaching a week, while the students have about thirty to thirty-five lessons a week, depending on the subjects (six or seven) they choose for examination. More or less one-third of the teaching time for Dutch language and literature is devoted to literature.

As can be seen in figure 4.1, more than one-third of the teaching time is devoted to the literature curriculum. Most of the schools in the survey allotted three lessons a week to the Dutch language and literature curriculum, so this

Figure 4.1: Language curriculum teaching time

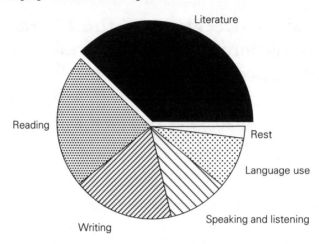

implies that about one hour a week is devoted to literature. Note that we present a general view, based on means from a survey: the differences between teachers are large! The time within the literature curriculum is spent on history of literature (39 per cent), in-class reading (24 per cent) and theory of literature (22 per cent). The curriculum is dominated by two general aims (see figure 4.2): to encourage reading pleasure and cultural literacy. General aims such as personal development, social awareness and aesthetic awareness obtained in general neutral (some more than neutral) support.

When we try to sketch the classroom situation by defining the attitude of the students towards the literature curriculum, it emerges from figure 4.3 that teachers feel that they have to teach to classes which are not interested in literature, nor in literature lessons: most of the students are defined by the teachers as almost non-readers of literature and most of them are regarded as having no insight into literature as a phenomenon. Only a very small number are defined as enthusiastic readers, and about half of the class is thought to be motivated for literature lessons.

We have already shown (figure 4.2) that several general aims for literature teaching are held by teachers. When we asked them which goal was best reflected in their teaching practice, it emerged that the teaching perspective 'literature as cultural literacy' guided their literature teaching the most. Aesthetic and social awareness were in fewer instances the focus of teaching. Personal development obtained the second highest degree of support.

Just as an example, we show in figure 4.5 that we defined relationships between perspectives on teaching and the content of the curriculum (see for a more extensive report Janssen and Rijlaarsdam, 1995). The proportion of attention devoted to history of literature and to literature theory is clearly related to the perspectives on teaching held by the teachers.

Figure 4.2: Importance of general aims

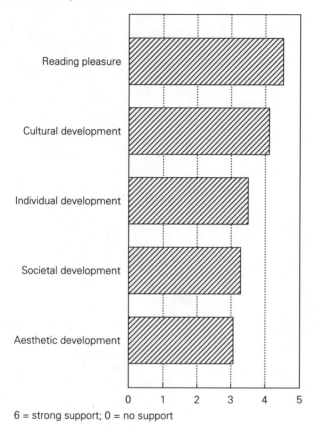

6 = strong support; 0 = no support

Evaluation of Literature Teaching

Despite the fact that teachers put a great deal of time into teaching literature (it takes up about a third of all the time spent on teaching Dutch), next to nothing is known about what good the students derive from this process. As part of a study to relate the output of teaching to the content and method of teaching, we applied an evaluation method developed by a Dutch psychologist, A.D. de Groot (1978 and 1980). He stated that one has to differentiate the type of evaluation according to the type of the relevant educational goal. Some goals can be measured by testing, others by demonstrating and others by communicating. Students can take tests of knowledge, can demonstrate their skills and can report about educational encounters like literature teaching (see also Eisner, 1986). According to De Groot, all desired teaching-learning effects should meet two conditions:

(i) the student should have learned something, in the sense of acquisition; the student can take the result with him, so to speak;

Figure 4.3:   Teachers about students' reading experience and motivation

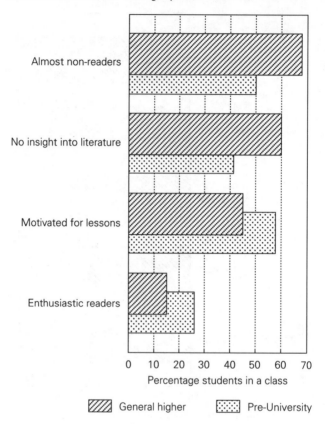

(ii)   the effect is his mental possession, which he can use according to his own decision, consciously and in freedom.

Of course, a student takes more from school than the desired teaching-learning effects. Conscious and unconscious influences by teachers and peers are part of the social situation which is education. These results of schooling are also learning effects, but we do not call them teaching-learning effects as long as the student himself does not know what he learned and why, as long as he is unable to take a position on these learning results. So we define a teaching-learning effect as a desired learning effect, which is to be characterized as a mental programme, acquired by the student as he learns, to be added to or inserted into, the total repertoire already available to the student.

Teaching aims do not include attitudinal aims because, although one can always hope, one cannot require that a student be interested in a school subject, for instance, or in literature in particular. The student is free to choose to be interested or not. The cognitive part of attitudes can be part of teaching: in teaching, it is not the case that students should be interested or not

Figure 4.4: Perspectives on teaching

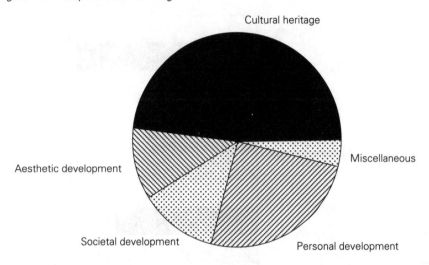

in literature, but that students learn what they want or feel, and how they can manage these interests and feelings. From this perspective, this set of teaching aims results in cognitive teaching-learning results. The results are about knowing what and knowing how, regarding yourself: knowledge about oneself and the skills one can display.

This point of view results in the fact that all learning results which correspond with legitimate teaching aims are to be described as acquired knowledge and skills about which a student possesses consciousness, and therefore can be reported by the student himself. Basically the reporting sentence is (De Groot, 1980):

> I have learned that . . .
> I have learned how . . .

And when affective teaching aims are involved:

> I have experienced that I . . .
> I found out that I . . .

If we accept that the result of education is not only the behaviour the students show (the performance), but the repertoire of behaviour the student has to his/her access, the next step is to ask the question as to how we can classify these learning results.

We can distinguish at least two types of learning experiences. The first type is the discovery of, the insight into, and the skill to apply rules. The second type is the discovery of, the insight into and the application of exceptions to the rules. Many learning processes consist of an alternation between the

Figure 4.5:   Dominance of sciences

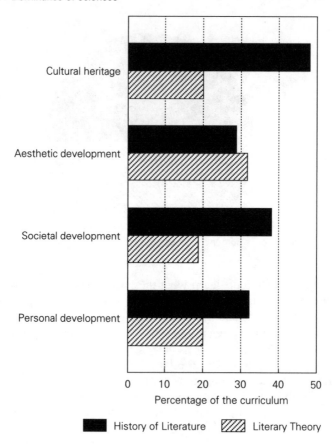

Percentage of the curriculum

■ History of Literature   ▨ Literary Theory

learning of rules and the learning of exceptions. First one detects a rule. Then a case in which the rule is not valid is discovered. Later on, one discovers that this case is an element of a class of exceptions to which the rule cannot be applied. Differentiation from the rule becomes a necessary step.

A second principle for classifying learning experiences is the object of learning: learning about oneself versus learning about the world. In the case of learning about oneself, learning results which have a personal character are involved: rules which can be applied to me, but not necessarily to others, and also exceptions to preconceptions. All in all, a simple two by two matrix of learning experiences can be designed: type of learning (rules versus exceptions) and object of learning (world versus oneself). When students report about their learning experiences, we can classify them into four categories (see Janssen and Rijlaarsdam, chapter 5 of this volume). This is a first step towards an instrument to collect and report data about what students learn from literature lessons.

Figure 4.6: Triangular model for contextual evaluation

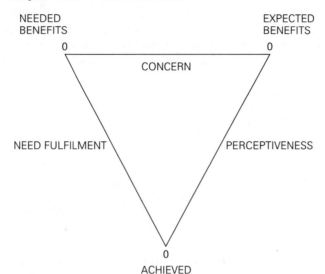

A Social Frame of Reference

Education is a social event. So is evaluation. Results of performance, collected in system or community A may be sufficient, regarding the demands of system A, but insufficient for system or community B (see Rijlaarsdam, 1992). One can substitute for system of community e.g. a class, a school, a school system, a region, a country, etc. Systems in which cultural literacy is very important will evaluate outcomes of literature teaching from another perspective than systems in which personal growth has been given priority. So evaluation has to be framed in the community or system: we do not only need to 'assess' students' performance or learning experiences, but also important features of the system or community involved in the evaluation of that experience. We apply the social framework of the triangular model of evaluation (Rijlaarsdam 1992; Janssen and Rijlaarsdam, 1992).

Figure 4.6 shows that we need three types of data. First of all, we require a description of the achieved benefits of the educational system: results of a knowledge test, skills assessment, reports of knowledge. Then we require a description of the needed benefits: what level of performance does the community need? The discrepancy between these two levels indicates the level of need fulfilment. We also require a description of the expected benefits. The discrepancy between the expected and the needed level of performance indicates the level of concern: the larger the discrepancy, the more concern is expressed. A comparison between the expected and achieved benefits indicates the level of perceptiveness of the community: the larger the discrepancy, the less the community seems to be aware of the actual results. It is clear that perceptiveness is an important characteristic of the respondents: when respondents express a low level of need fulfilment (needed benefits are higher than actual benefits) and their level of perceptiveness is low (achieved benefits are higher than expected benefits), then one may state that a large part of the concern the community indicates may be the 'whingeing factor' of this community.

Instrumentation

We used 'learner reports' in order to collect the learning experiences of students and a similar instrument to determine teachers' intended objectives and their estimates of the product of their teaching of literature.

The instrument for obtaining learning experiences from the students was divided into four sections (see Janssen and Rijlaarsdam, chapter 5 in this volume). The instrument contains for each of these sections starting sentences, to help students to generate their learning experiences (see appendix).

We found nine teachers who were known to teach literature in a style clearly not 'middle of the road', and asked them for their collaboration. These teachers were presented with three questionnaires:

1 **About what they offered the student in their teaching of literature.**

   This questionnaire consisted of a series of multiple choice questions about the content and form of their literature lessons: the number of hours devoted to literature, the methods used, the kind of work the students did, and so on. We also used this questionnaire to collect certain background information on the teachers: age, experience, etc.

2 **About their expectations regarding the benefits of their teaching of literature (expected benefits).**

   This questionnaire was of an open nature: we asked teachers to put themselves in their students' shoes and write down the learning experiences that they expected of them. The questionnaire was divided into the same four sections we used in the students' report. We asked the teachers also to write down their negative expectations: possible learning experiences of their students that the teachers disliked.

3 **About desired learning effects (needed benefits).**

   Here we asked them to write down learning effects that they themselves considered desirable, without regard to the constraints they experienced in their daily practice, and to write down learning effects that they considered undesirable. This questionnaire was also divided into the four sections we mentioned before.

In order to collect data about the achieved benefits, we asked the students of these nine teachers, confining ourselves to the top two forms of grammar schools, to write a learner report. For each teacher fifteen students were selected at random, except that over the whole sample we ensured that the numbers of boys and girls were equal. Our data collection then consisted of more than 100 statements from the teachers about the needed benefits, 267 statements by teachers on the expected benefits and 1278 learning sentences from students on the actual benefits. When analyzing the learning experiences reported by both teachers and students in their reports, we modified the classification scheme for the objectives of literature teaching drawn up by Purves (1971; see for an extensive description of modifications Janssen and Rijlaarsdam 1990b). Purves's scheme has two axes. Along one of these lies the content of instruction in literature, on the other various behaviours that are required. We present our categories below, illustrated with learning sentences from students' reports.

Content

Literary works
This category refers to statements of students who have learned something about (specific) authors, poems, stories, novels, plays or about literary texts in general. Examples:

> 'I have discovered that Dutch literature is "grave", "a drip" and "old fashioned".'
> 'I have learned that poems are exceedingly boring.'
> 'I have come to know more writers and books.'

Literary backgrounds
This category refers to statements about authors' biographies and literary historical information. This category also contains statements about the production of literature (how are books made, what does a publisher do) or about the reception of literature (how are literary works received by the press, how did people formerly react to literature). Examples:

> 'I have learned that Wolkers (a Dutch author) is not a dirty fellow.'
> 'I have learned what is meant by Romanticism.'
> 'I have learned how literature comes into being.'

Non-literary backgrounds
This refers to background information that is not strictly literary, but is more general in nature, such as cultural, social or political background information. Examples:

> 'I have learned that in the old days many people could not read or write.'
> 'I have learned how life was in mediaeval times, because of all the chivalric epics we read.'
> 'I have learned that the beginning of the nineteenth century was a time of cosiness and hominess.'

Analysis and interpretation

This refers to story and poetry analysis, or terminology used in analysis (perspective, theme, motives, rhyme). Also included in this category are sentences about the act of interpretation. Examples:

> 'I have learned that analyzing stories is more difficult than I thought.'
> 'I have learned that a sonnet consists of fourteen lines and a particular rhyme scheme.'
> 'I have learned that one story can generate several interpretations.'

Text and reader

This category is about the relationship of the literary work to the reader. By this we mean all learning experiences in which the student says that he has learned something about his own reading behaviour or that of others. Also sentences about a particular relation between the student-reader and a literary text were included in this category. Examples:

> 'I have noticed that I have difficulties in concentrating while reading.'
> 'I have learned that some books made me sad, while others made me glad.'
> 'I learned a lot about who I am by reading.'

Use of literary language

This included all sentences about language activities related to literature lessons, be it the production of literary texts or communicating about literature (projects). Examples:

> 'I have noticed that I enjoy writing stories.'
> 'I have learned how to prepare a speech about a book.'

General use of language

This relates to learning to write, read, speak, listen and observe in general, without special reference to literature. Examples:

> 'I have learned to use paragraphs in written texts.'
> 'I have discovered that my spelling is worse than I thought.'
> 'I have experienced that I find it hard to express my opinion during a discussion.'

Collecting information

This is also a general category involving sentences about searching for secondary literature about books and authors and the use of libraries. Examples:

> 'I know how to find extracts.'
> 'I have experienced that I like to walk around libraries.'

Literature lesson
Students quite often made evaluative statements about the teaching of literature, particularly about the obligatory reading list. Examples:

'I have discovered that literature lessons are not that boring.'
'I learned that I hate the reading list.'
'I learned that you can't fake: the teacher always found out when I pretended to have read a book.'

Behaviour

Knowledge
'Knowledge' not only refers to the reproduction of factual information, but also to having an understanding of complex phenomena and structures. Examples:

'I have learned how people in the old days thought about literature.'
'I now know what literature is about.'

Skill
'Skill' refers to students knowing *how* something has to be done and/or having mastered a certain skill. Examples:

'I have learned how to analyze a story.'
'I have noticed that I am able to analyze a story.'

Positive attitude
This category refers to favourable or positive opinions about something. The student finds something 'nice', 'pleasant', 'amusing'. Qualifications such as 'easy', 'useful', 'interesting', 'important' or 'beautiful' also reflect a positive opinion. Examples:

'I have noticed that I like reading books.'
'I think literary history is fairly important.'

Negative attitude
The counterpart of the last category: the student dislikes something, or finds something boring, annoying, useless, unimportant, stupid or ugly. Examples:

'I have learned that literature lessons are a waste of time.'
'I have learned that only the teacher appreciates literature.'

Other behaviour
The remainder of students' statements: among other things statements that are too vague to be placed in one of the other categories.

Figure 4.7:   Classification scheme

CONTENT	BEHAVIOUR				
	Knowledge	*Skill*	*Positive attitude*	*Negative attitude*	*Other behaviour*
Literary works					
Literary contextual information					
Non-literary contextual information					
Literary theory, analysis, interpretation					
Relationship literary work/reader					
Use of literary language					
General use of language					
Collecting information					
Literature lesson					
Other contents					

Figure 4.7 shows the classification scheme we used in this study (see Janssen and Rijlaarsdam, chapter 5 in this volume, for an updated version).

Evaluation of Learning Results

In this section, we present the learning benefits, and the framing of these results in a relevant social context: the desirable and expected benefits formulated by the teachers of the students involved in this study.

As a basis, we report here (see table 4.1) the learning categories which make what we call the core curriculum of students. It shows the most frequent learning sentences responses (up to about 80 per cent) in figures, per thousand returns. We present here the results of the cells.

The question now is: how to interpret this kind of data? Should we be content with these results? Are curriculum aims fulfilled? So now we will frame the results in the triangular model of evaluation. Note that we asked the teachers of the students involved in this study also to write learner reports. We asked them to write a learner report they expected to read from their students, which indicates the Expected Level of outcomes, and we asked them to write a learner report they would like to read from their students, when ideal curriculum circumstances were reached, which indicates the Needed Level of outcomes. We will report these data in effect sizes (Cohen, 1988). Effect sizes are obtained by the ratio of the differences of means by the pooled standard deviation. The standardization provides the possibility of comparing the different measures and indicators directly. Cohen formulated rules for interpretation of the size of these measures: an effect size lower than .30 is called a small effect, an effect size larger than .80 is called a large effect, and sizes in between are medium effect sizes. We will report the results on the main categories of learning, rather than of all possible combinations of our coding scheme.

Table 4.1: *The actual benefits of literature teaching. Categories of learning which make 80 per cent of the learning sentences reported in figures, per thousand returns*

LEARNING CATEGORY	Promilles
1 Positive attitude to literary works	118
2 Knowledge about literary contextual information	117
3 Negative attitude about lit. works	71
4 Knowledge about lit. works	65
5 Negative attitude to lit. lessons	41
6 Skill of literary theory	40
7 Knowledge of lit. theory	35
8 Knowledge of relationship work-reader	32
9 Positive attitude to use of lit. language	32
10 Positive attitude to lit. lesson	32
11 Pos. attitude to lit. contextual information	30
12 Skill in use of lit. language	30
13 Knowledge of non-literary contextual information	29
14 Other contents/other activities	28
15 Lit. works/other activities	26
16 Skill in general use of language	25
17 Positive attitude relationship work-reader	25
18 Negative attitude to lit. contextual information	23

Concerns about the Literature Curriculum: The C-indicator

If we relate the ideal curriculum to the expected outcome, we have an indication of the concerns. A discrepancy between the two measures indicates concern. When the ideal results are higher than the Expected Results, then goals are worth striving for, and these goals need extra attention because teachers think that goals are not achieved.

In most cases, in education and in life also, one feels a discrepancy between the ideal and the world: there is always something left to strive for. We always want something more and better and are never fully satisfied about the outcomes of our lessons. So in this cluster of outcomes we generally find this set of data: one's Ideal Curriculum should produce more learning sentences in these fields of outcomes than the curriculum (and the pupils) one has to work with in practical circumstances. So one is not satisfied in this case.

Figure 4.8 shows the results for the Concern-indicator. Two clusters of data can be distinguished: positive effect sizes (upper part) and negative effect sizes (lower part). A positive size of the Concern-indicator implies a feeling of 'curriculum in danger'. Learning categories such as Literary Background, Text and Reader, Knowledge, are categories 'in danger': teachers expect a lower number of learning sentences than they would like to achieve. Note that the learning category Negative Attitude is a negative category. In this category, teachers expect to find more sentences than they would like to find, so this category is in danger too. The Concern scores in the learning category Literature Lessons indicate also a concern: teachers expect more sentences about this category than they would like to find in learning reports. So the only aspects of the literature curriculum teachers feel satisfied about are Literary Works,

Figure 4.8: Literature curriculum concern

Categories of learning

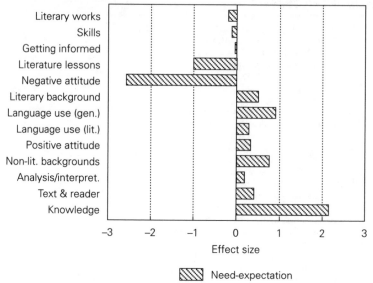

Need-expectation

Skills and Getting Informed: the discrepancies between Ideal and Expected results are rather small. Note that there is no category with a lower need than the expected level, which would indicate that the curriculum results in outcomes which are not very important (any more, any longer). In total, we have to conclude that there is a strong feeling of concern about the outcome of the literature curriculum in teachers: they feel they do not reach the needed level of outcome.

The Accuracy of Observed Benefits by Relevant Respondents: The P-indicator

The second step in the triangular model of evaluation is to relate the Expected Level with the Actual Level of Outcome. This comparison gives an impression of the accuracy or the perceptiveness of the relevant respondents: the Perceptiveness Indicator. The question to be answered is: to what extent are teachers aware of the outcome of the curriculum? When the indicator reaches a positive value (see figure 4.9), then the Achieved Level outscores the Expected Level, which means that the Expected Level is too low. When the indicator is negative, then the Expected Level is too high.

In figure 4.9 we see six learning categories with a positive Perceptiveness Indicator: Literary Works, Skills, Literary Background, Language Use (in general as well as related to Literature) and Positive Attitude. Teachers have too

Figure 4.9: *Literature curriculum perceptiveness*

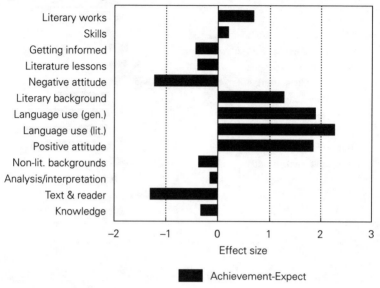

low expectations regarding these learning categories: students report more learning sentences than teachers expect.

The other seven categories show a negative P-indicator, of which two are large: Negative Attitude and Text and Reader. In the case of Negative Attitude, the negative P-indicator indicates a positive effect, because the learning category itself is negative. The indicator here implies that students report a smaller number of learning sentences on Negative Attitude than teachers expect. The resulting learning category with a large negative P-indicator implies that teachers expect more learning sentences than pupils actually reported. So in this category teachers are non-perceptive too, but in this case they overestimate the actual level: the output of the curriculum is lower than teachers expect.

We have to conclude that the P-indicator reaches a high level in several cases, implying that teachers misperceive the outcome of the Literature Curriculum. Misperception of the actual level of outcome is important in cases where Expected outcome and Needed outcome show a large discrepancy. In the latter case, teachers indicate an unhappy feeling about the curriculum. But when this unhappy feeling goes together with a misperceived level of outcome, then the feeling is unnecessarily negative. Therefore we have to combine the P-indicator with the C-indicator (see figure 4.10): this combination indicates the level of 'whingeing': when relevant respondents complain about the benefits of the curriculum while the benefits are better than expected, such complaints are not based on 'facts' and are inaccurate, therefore indicating in the 'whingeness' level of the social group involved.

Figure 4.10: *Literature curriculum perceptiveness and concern*

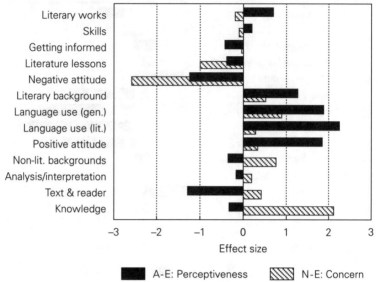

Concern Related to Perceptiveness: The Whingeing Factor

The first cluster is formed by Literary Works and Skills. We see in figure 4.10, for both Literary Works and Skills, the Ideal Results are a bit lower than the Expected Results. So, teachers would be happy if pupils wrote down fewer sentences about Literary Works and about Skills then they expected pupils to do. However, in fact the pupils report a lot more learning sentences than the teachers feared. So teachers probably are disappointed about these results.

The second cluster consists of Literary Lessons and Negative Attitude. Of course, teachers don't like remarks about the Literature Lessons themselves as an output of their education: lessons are a means, not a goal in themselves. And of course, teachers do not desire negative attitudes to Literature as an outcome of their teaching. In fact, pupils report much fewer outcomes in these two fields than teachers expected. This is an outcome that must satisfy teachers in one respect: happily the dissension teachers felt about the negative attitudes about Literature, induced by the curriculum, can be attributed in part to a misestimation of the actual reported output. Their image of their practice is too negative. In another respect this outcome is enough to make us think about the strengths of social and cultural pressure: the negative atmosphere in society concerning the quality and outcomes of the literary curriculum seems to distort the observations of the teachers: they are wrongly too negative about their practice.

The third cluster consists of Literary Background Knowledge, Language

Skills (in respect to Literature and for general purposes) and Positive Attitudes. In fact, pupils not only reported more learning effects than teachers expected, they reported more than teachers hoped to receive under Ideal Circumstances. In this case, the teachers will be satisfied: their practice attains more than they expected and they dared to hope for. This last observation is difficult to interpret. The C-indicator in all four cases is many times smaller than the P-indicator. The level of concern, in other words, is smaller than the level of misperception. We do not know what role the misperception plays in the concern: are teachers concerned as a result of the misperception?

The fourth cluster consists of Non-Literary Background, Analysis and Interpretation, Text and Reader, and Knowledge. In this cluster teachers express their concern, and would like to find more learning sentences than they expect; in fact, students wrote fewer sentences then teachers expected. So this cluster consists of real problematic learning categories. In the three cases with a low level of misperception (Non-Literary Backgrounds, Analysis and Interpretation and Knowledge), the interpretation is rather clear: the concern the teachers feel is a real one. The learning category Text and Reader is interesting because of the relatively large P-indicator: teachers are not aware of the low number of learning sentences in this category, while they hope to find more of them in ideal circumstances. The actual need, in other words, is larger than the felt need.

Do the Benefits Fulfil the Contextual Needs? The N-indicator

The fourth step is to study the Need-fulfilment Indicator, which related the needed and the actual level of Outcome (see figure 4.11).

Here we see that in most cases achievement outscores the felt need: students wrote more sentences than needed, according to teachers, in the learning categories Literary Works, Skills, Literature Lessons, Negative Attitude, Literary Background, Language Use (2x) and Positive Attitude. They wrote too few about Non-literary Background, Analysis and Interpretation, Text and Reader and Knowledge. So it seems as if the curriculum performs better than needed in some cases, and worse than needed in other cases. But now we have to relate the needed level to the level of accuracy: the Perceptiveness level. We combine these two indicators in figure 4.12.

Now we see that in most cases the sign of the two indicators is the same: the Needed and the Perceived Level have the same sign. So the teachers did not expect to find this number of sentences on Positive Attitude for instance, and they did not express a need to find this number either. Because of the large P-indicator, we may conclude that in the cases of Literary Works, Skills, Getting Informed, Literary Backgrounds, Language Use (2x) and Positive Attitude, the Literature Curriculum reaches the needed level, if we correct the Needed Level for Misperceived Level of outcome. From those categories, teachers felt concerned about Literary Backgrounds, Language Use (2x) and Positive Attitude. This concern (see figure 4.8) seems to be unnecessary: the

Figure 4.11: Literature curriculum need fulfilment

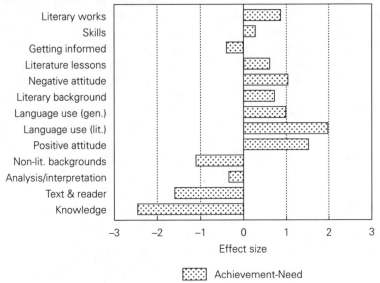

Categories of learning

Effect size

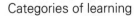 Achievement-Need

concerns teachers express are based on a misperception of the outcomes: the outcomes are much better than teachers expected, and even outscore the Needed Level. Teachers seem to adjust the Needed Level to a misperceived low level of Expected outcomes. The other three categories, Literary Works, Skills and Getting Informed were of no concern to the teachers (see figure 4.8). The Needed Level is almost as large as the Perceived Level. For Literary Works the Perceived Level is Misperceived, so for this category the problem of interpretation is raised: does the curriculum focus too much on Literary Works because the number of learning sentences is larger than the Needed Level, or is the Needed Level set too low because of a misperception of the Expected Level?

In figure 4.12 two clusters are left for interpretation. In one cluster, consisting of Literature Lessons and Negative Attitude, more sentences are found than needed, and fewer sentences are found than expected. Note that for these categories, the Concern-indicator was relatively large (see figure 4.8). Teachers expected more (negative) sentences than they would like to find. So the actual Level is better than expected, and better than needed. The concern expressed seems to be completely unnecessary.

The last cluster, consisting of Non-Literary Backgrounds, Analysis and Interpretation, Text and Reader and Knowledge, is characterized by a lower level of achievement than expected and needed. For Text and Reader, we may conclude that teachers largely misperceived the Expected Level, and, therefore, the low number of sentences is a larger concern than they expressed

Figure 4.12:   Literature curriculum perceptiveness & fulfilment

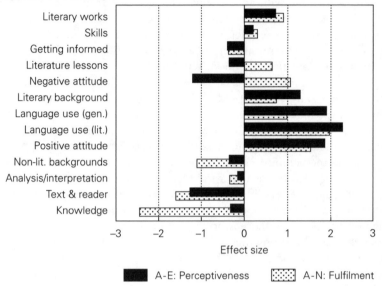

(see figure 4.8). This may be stated as a hidden concern: teachers did not express their concern, but this seems to be a mistake, because students did not report many sentences in this category. For curriculum designers, this fact will be difficult to tackle. When they try to focus more on the category Text and Reader, teachers would not buy these text books, because they did not feel that the curriculum should be more focussed on Text and Reader.

For the three categories left, the P-indicator is relatively small, so the negative sign of the Fulfilment indicator should be of concern: the curriculum does not reach the Needed Level, and the Needed Level is not invalidated by misperception of the Expected Level. So teachers will try to focus more on these categories. In the case of Knowledge, this movement will be the most striking one: teachers expressed a large concern, they did not misperceive the expected level, but the Actual Level seemed to be lower than they expected.

Conclusion

We started out with a desire to demonstrate that the use of learner reports can be a valid instrument for evaluating learning outcomes. By asking teachers to predict what their pupils would write and comparing these predictions with the facts, the learning experiences, we obtain indicators of the degree to which the teaching concerned is achieving its objectives. On the basis of such an evaluation individual teachers can adjust their teaching.

Such an evaluation might also have the effect of making people's view of literature teaching less gloomy than at present. There is nothing worse than teaching something without knowing what good your teaching is doing, especially if you have the impression that the negative effects are large. We have seen that teachers are worried about negative attitudes caused by their teaching of literature, but pupils report a negative attitude much less often than teachers fear. And they mention 1001 things that teachers miss as possible learning effects. Are teachers so uncertain about the effects of their teaching that they not only fail to predict them correctly but also have excessively negative expectations about the attitudes that students form as a result of them? We hope that with this instrument and its progeny we will be giving teachers a clearer insight into what their pupils get out of literature teaching.

This demonstration of the triangular model of evaluation intended to argue, on the one hand, that gathering facts about the benefits of the literature curriculum is possible by using learner reports and, on the other hand, that these data are not enough. Collecting data about performance and knowledge is useless, when there is no frame of reference. Education is a social act, as is defining educational needs. The triangular model of evaluation provides such contextual information. Which groups are chosen to provide the contextual framework depends on the aim of evaluation. Several groups participate in the communicative community. We used teachers in this study, but what about parents, employers, administrators? Are teachers more perceptive than parents, for instance? Are decision-makers well equipped (perceptive to actual benefits) to define nationwide educational aims? The triangular model of evaluation provides a basis for a rational discussion about the benefits and aims of education and of literature teaching in particular.

The most striking result in this chapter is that even the teachers who get everyday information about the performances of their pupils and do not have an adequate picture of the actual performance level in the domain of language skills. Regularly reflecting on what one expects to find and being confronted with the actual data, can help teachers (and society in general) to get more grip on reality. It could lead to more realistic goalsetting and less whingeing about the performance of the education system.

References

COHEN, J. (1988) *Statistical Power Analysis for the Behavioral Sciences* (2nd ed.), Hillsdale, NJ, Lawrence Erlbaum Associates.

GROOT, A.D. DE (1978) 'Wat neemt de leerling mee van onderwijs? Gedragsrepertoires, programma's, kennis-en-vaardigheden' ('What do students take with them from education? Behavioural repertoires, programmes, knowledge-and-skills'), *Handboek onderwijspraktijk*, afl, 2, januari.

GROOT, A.D. DE (1980) 'Over leerevaringen en leerdoelen' ('About Learning Experiences and Learning Aims'), *Handboek Onderwijspraktijk*, **10**, 3.2. Gro. B. 1 — Gro. B. 18.

JANSSEN, T.M. and RIJLAARSDAM, G.C.W. (1990a) 'Opbrengsten van literatuuronderwijs: Een vooronderzoek' (Benefits of Literature Teaching: Preliminary Research), *Spiegel*, **8**, 2, pp. 29–47.

JANSSEN, T.M. and RIJLAARSDAM, G.C.W. (1990b) 'What pupils learn from literature teaching in the Netherlands' in HAYHOE, M. and PARKER, S. (Eds) *Reading and Response*, Milton Keynes, Open University Press, pp. 94–106.

JANSSEN, T. and RIJLAARSDAM, G. (1992a) 'Approaches to the teaching of literature: A survey of literary education in secondary schools in the Netherlands', paper presented at the Third IGEL conference, May, Memphis, Tennessee.

JANSSEN, T. and RIJLAARSDAM, G. (1992b) 'Het learner report in de praktijk van de bovenbouw' ('Learner Reports in Teaching Practices in Higher Secondary Education') in MOOR, W. DE and VAN WOERKOM, M. (Eds) *Literaire Competentie. Het doel van Literatuuronderwijs* (*Literary competence: The Aim of Literature Teaching*), Den Haag, NBLC, pp. 197–208.

JANSSEN, T. and RIJLAARSDAM, G. (1995) 'Approaches to the teaching of literature: A survey of literary education in secondary schools in the Netherlands' in KREUTZ, R.J. and MACNEALY, M.S. (Eds) *Empirical Approaches to Literature and Aesthetics*, Norwood, NJ, Ablex Publishing Corporation.

PURVES, A.C. (1971) 'Evaluation of learning in literature' in BLOOM, B.S., HASTINGS, J.T. and MADAUS, G.F. (Eds) *Handbook on Formative and Summative Evaluation of Student Learning*, New York, McGraw-Hill.

RIJLAARSDAM, G. and JANSSEN T. (1992) 'Reflectie op de literaire competentie van de leerlingen aan de hand van leerverslagen' ('Reflection on students' literary competence, based on learner reports') in MOOR, W. DE and VAN WOERKOM, M. (Eds) *Literaire Competentie. Het doel van Literatuuronderwijs*, Den Haag, NBLC, pp. 209–22.

RIJLAARSDAM, G. (1992) 'The triangular model for intra- and intercontextual evaluation of written composition' in HELBO, A. (Ed.) *Evaluation and Language Testing*, Bern, Peter Lang, pp. 259–74.

ZWARTS, M., RIJLAARSDAM, G.C.W., JANSSENS, F., WOLFHAGEN, I., VELDHUIJZEN, N. and WESDORP, H. (1990) *Balans van het Taalonderwijs aan het einde van de basisschool.* Uitkomsten van de eerste taalpeiling einde basisonderwijs. (Weighing language curriculum higher forms of primary education. Results of the first national assessment study), PPON-reeks nr. 2, Arnhem, CITO.

ZWARTS, M. and RIJLAARSDAM, G. (1991) *Verantwoording van de Taalpeiling Einde Basisonderwijs 1988.* (Backgrounds of National Assessment Study of Language Teaching), PPON-Rapport nr. 6, Arnhem, CITO.

Appendix: Instrument to collect learning sentences

Section A

I have learned from my literature lessons that/how . . .
You may have learned things so that you know general rules, facts, techniques. You know how something should be done, how something is constructed.
Introductory phrases:

> I have learned/noticed/discovered/now know that . . .
> because/then/in those days/for example . . .
> I have learned/noticed/discovered/now know how . . .
> because/then/in those days/for example . . .

Write below and on the next sheet as many learning sentences that apply to you as possible.
(. . . . .)

Section B

I have learned from my literature lessons that it is not the case that . . .
You may have learned or discovered that there are exceptions: things have sometimes turned out differently from what you had expected.
Introductory phrases:

> I have learned/noticed/discovered/now know that
> it is not true that . . .
> it is not the case that . . .
> there are also . . .
> not all . . .
> whereas I used to think that . . .

Write below and on the next sheet as many learning sentences that apply to you as possible.
(. . . . .)

Section C

I have learned from my literature lessons that I . . .
You may have learned or discovered things about yourself. About what kind of person you are, how you react to things, how you work best, what you like, what you dislike.
Introductory phrases:

I have learned/discovered/noticed/now know
that I think . . . ,
that I am good/bad at . . .
that I like/hate . . .
that the best way I can do . . . is to . . .
because/then/for example . . .

Write below and on the next sheet as many learning sentences that apply to
you as possible.
(. . . . .)

Section D

I have learned from my literature lessons that I do not . . .
You may have found out some exceptions about yourself. Everything you
have discovered by way of exceptions about yourself: that you are not always
as you thought you were, that you thought you were always like this or that,
or that you always acted in such and such a manner, but that it has turned out
that this is not always the case. That you like other things than you thought
you did, that you react to things differently from the way you thought you did,
that you work differently from the way you thought you did. What kind of
exceptions about yourself have you learned from your literature lessons?
Introductory phrases:

I have learned/discovered/noticed/now know that it is not true/not the
case that I always . . .
I never . . .
I always like/dislike . . .
I am good/bad at . . .
I always have to tackle . . . by . . . , but that I can also . . .
whereas I used to think that I . . .

Write below and on the next sheet as many learning sentences that apply to
you as possible.
(. . . . .)

5 Students as Self-assessors: Learning Experiences of Literature Teaching in Secondary Schools

Tanja Janssen and Gert Rijlaarsdam

Introduction

What are the effects of literature teaching? What do students actually learn from it? These are difficult questions, we admit, but nevertheless questions that deserve attempts at an answer. Literature has always been a serious, sacrosanct part of the curriculum of secondary education. In the Netherlands literature takes up about a third of all time spent on mother tongue teaching in secondary schools.[1] The educational practice varies widely, because schools and individual teachers have as yet the freedom to determine the contents of the curriculum themselves (Janssen and Rijlaarsdam, 1995).

In recent years, however, the position of literature has been put under pressure by an increasing emphasis on the socioeconomic function of education. In order to improve the tie-up between secondary education and higher vocational training the Dutch government intends to reshape the curriculum for secondary schools. New school subjects will be introduced and functional and communicative language skills will take the upper hand, at the expense of literary knowledge and skills. In the near future teachers will have less time at their disposal for teaching literature and fewer possibilities to establish their own emphases with regard to the content of their teaching (Witte, 1995).[2]

At the same time there is a growing concern about the decline of reading and lack of 'cultural literacy' of young people. In the media one regularly finds complaints about the falling standards of literary education or anecdotal reports about students' supposed lack of literary competence. Teachers in particular are concerned. They often seem to be uncertain about the effects of their teaching. Their main fears are that their students will dislike the reading of literature as a result of their lessons and that students will find the lessons vague and pointless (Janssen and Rijlaarsdam, 1990a). We think it is important to collect evidence to document the (un)truth of such complaints and, eventually, to provide a clear insight into what students gain from literature teaching.

As already stated, literature as a school subject is not a homogeneous entity. Different goals and approaches can be perceived in the self-reported educational practices of teachers, as is shown by results of a national survey

(Janssen and Rijlaarsdam, 1995). Some teachers consider the promotion of 'cultural literacy' of students as the main goal of their literature lessons. These teachers tend to spend more time teaching literary history and discussing the 'classics' of Dutch literature than other teachers. Their teaching method also tends to be rather traditional: they lecture predominantly, while students listen and take notes.

Other teachers see promoting the 'personal development' of students as the main goal of their teaching. Reading and discussing literature is viewed by them as a means to the further personal, emotional growth of students as individuals. These teachers tend to pay less attention to literary history and other background-information and more attention to students' attitudes and own experiences in connection with reading literature. In order to stimulate the personal responses of students to literature, class discussion and small group work are the preferred teaching methods.

The question is whether these different approaches to the teaching of literature do indeed culminate in different learning outcomes for students. Is the perceived discrepancy between 'cultural literacy' and 'personal development' also reflected in the results that are achieved? Or are the benefits of these different approaches more or less the same? Measuring results of literature teaching is not an easy undertaking. The objectives are stated in such general, idealistic terms ('cultural literacy', 'personal development'), that any attempt to measure learning outcomes is considered to be invalid. Yet in recent years efforts have been made to determine learning outcomes for other, comparable school subjects. With reference to De Groot's (1978) theory about learning effects and Eisner's (1969) distinction between 'educational encounters' and 'instructional objectives', Van der Kamp (1980) carried out research into the learning experiences of students who followed art classes. In his study he used a form of self-assessment: students wrote down their learning experiences in a so called 'learner report'. Following Van der Kamp several others have used the learner report for educational and research purposes (see Van Kesteren, 1989, for an overview).

In this chapter we report on a small-scale study to examine the effects of two approaches to the teaching of literature: a cognitive ('cultural literacy') approach and a more affective ('personal development') approach.[3] To determine the learning outcomes we used learner reports. Our questions were:

(a) Are students able to report on their learning experiences in a so called learning report?

(b) May we consider the learner report to be a valid instrument to determine learning outcomes of literature teaching?

(c) If so, are there any differences in learning outcomes between a more cognitive (cultural literacy) approach and a more affective (personal development) approach to teaching literature?

(d) If so, to what extent can differences in learning outcomes be explained by features of the educational practice?

In order to answer the first two questions, a pilot-study was performed in which nine teachers of Dutch and their students participated. To answer the last two questions, we focussed on two teachers: one representative of the cultural literacy approach ('Chantal') and one representative of the personal development approach ('Alex').

The Instrument

The learner report is a form of self-report or self-evaluation. Students are asked to indicate what they have learned from literature lessons, either by making themselves statements starting with 'I have learned that . . .' or by (dis)agreeing with a given series of statements about possible learning effects.

De Groot (1978 and 1980) distinguishes four domains of learning experiences:

A Rules concerning the world: to learn general rules, facts, techniques, things that always have to be this or that way.
B Exceptions concerning the world: to learn exceptions about the world, things that turn out differently from what was expected.
C Rules concerning oneself: to learn general rules, facts, insights about oneself, about how one is, how one reacts, what one likes or dislikes.
D Exceptions about oneself: to learn exceptions about oneself, things about oneself that turn out differently from what was expected.

The four domains are presented below, in figure 5.1.

Figure 5.1:   De Groot's four domains of learning experiences

	Rules	**Exceptions**
World	A	B
Self	C	D

According to De Groot, traditional achievement tests are limited to domain A, focusing on knowledge and skills that can easily be demonstrated by students and/or objectively measured. The domains C and D refer to self-knowledge and insight, personal experiences that cannot be demonstrated or objectively measured, but that can be reported by students. The learner report pretends to tap all four kinds of learning, but seems to be especially adequate to track down learning experiences in the domains C and D. These learning experiences may vary widely from student to student. Learner reports reflect not only the knowledge and skills that are explicitly transferred to students (the 'formal' curriculum), but also part of the 'hidden curriculum'. Students' reports can make visible what is left unsaid, what remains implicit in education (for a more extensive discussion of De Groot's theory, see Rijlaarsdam and Janssen, chapter 4 in this volume).

However, some have serious doubts about the reliability of the learner report (Van Kesteren, 1989). The reliability of the instrument strongly depends on the willingness of students to give an honest, faithful report of their learning experiences. Students may be able to report on what they have learnt, but there is no guarantee that what they report is true and not something they make up in order to give the teacher/researcher a favourable impression of themselves. Therefore, the instrument should only be used diagnostically (preferably anonymously) and not for examination purposes. If serious consequences for students are involved (like failing an exam), the chances of a faithful report are probably diminished.

The learner report can be used in different ways: individually or in groups, in an oral or written form, in an open or closed format (Van der Kamp, 1980; Van Kesteren, 1989). In our study we chose a written, open format. Our instrument contains:

— an introduction, presenting the purpose of the study;
— multiple choice questions with regard to reading habits, reading interests and preferences of the student;
— examples of learning experiences of students in other subject areas (art and writing);
— an explanation of the four domains of learning experiences;
— two blank sheets for each domain (A, B, C and D), preceded by 'introductory phrases'.

In figure 5.2 part of the learner report (section C) is presented.

Figure 5.2: One section of the learner report

Section C:
From the literature lessons I have learned that I . . .

You may have learned or discovered things about yourself. About what kind of person you are, how you react to things, how you work best, what you like, what you dislike.
Introductory phrases:
— I have learned/discovered/noticed/now know that
    I think . . .
    I am good/bad at . . .
    I like/hate . . .
    the best way I can do . . . is to . . .
because/then/for example . . .
Write below and on the next sheet as many learning sentences that you can think of.

Before students wrote their report, the researcher explained the purpose of the study and talked with the students about the contents of the literature classes they had followed. It was emphasized that the respondents remained anonymous and that there were no right or wrong answers. Writing the report took students about half-an-hour.

Testing the Learner Report

In a preliminary 'known-group-validity' study we tested the learner report as a research instrument.[4] The 'known group' consisted of nine teachers we knew ourselves or who were known by others to teach literature in a non-average way. In a written questionnaire the teachers were asked what their goals and methods were with regard to the teaching of literature. The results confirmed their different orientations, some of them emphasizing literary history, while others preferred a 'text studying' or 'text experiencing' approach.[5] We then asked students of each teacher to write a learner report. For each teacher fifteen learner reports were selected at random to be analyzed. These reports contained about 1300 statements on the benefits of literature lessons.

The statements of the students were analyzed, using a modified version of the classification scheme drawn up by Purves (1971). Two dimensions were distinguished: 'Behaviour' and 'Content', each sub-divided into categories. The main categories of Behaviour were: 'knowledge', 'skills' and 'attitudes'. Content was divided into nine categories, including among other things: 'literary works', 'literary contextual information', 'non-literary (social or cultural) contextual information', 'literary theory' and 'relationship literary text/reader' (see Rijlaarsdam and Janssen, chapter 4 in this volume).

Each statement in the learning reports was coded by two research assistants on both dimensions. Then, the proportion of learning experiences in each cell of the classification scheme was determined.

Our first question was whether students were able to write down their learning experiences. This question could be answered in the affirmative. Although students indicated that they found it a difficult task, most of them came up with a series of statements that made sense. Below we give one example, to illustrate what a learner report may look like.

Quotations from one of the learner reports in the pilot study

Section A. Rules concerning the world
  I have learned to recognize different styles of writing by authors.
  I have discovered that almost every literary school is a response to a preceding one.
  I have learned to notice the finite form of verbs in a book to know what kind of narrator the writer is using.
  I have learned through the years above all to read and listen critically.
  I have learned which books I like to read, namely books in which animals play a large part.
  That's why I like Koolhaas (Dutch author of animal stories) so much.

Section C. Rules concerning oneself
I have learned that I sometimes find it a bit exaggerated to fully unravel a book. Looking behind everything a writer writes, that is something I don't believe in. Maybe I have too much common sense.
I have learned from myself and my circle of acquaintances that everyone finds in a book the meaning he/she wants to find. So you can't make rules for that.

Most statements were found in the first section of the report, section A 'Rules concerning the world'. Apparently, the order in which the sections in the report are presented influences the number of statements students produce in each section. This was confirmed by Janssen and Rijlaarsdam (1992). To eliminate this effect, it is advisable to use different versions of the report, varying the order of the sections. The versions may be distributed at random.

Our second question concerned the validity of the learner report. Is the instrument sensitive enough to reveal differences in the perceived benefits from different forms of literature teaching? If in the analyzed statements of the students we had found traces of the differences between the teachers, this would substantiate the claim to validity of the learner report. Our previous knowledge of the teachers and the results of the written questionnaire made it likely that the teachers did indeed differ from each other with regard to the content of their literature lessons.

In order to trace differences in the analyzed learning outcomes between the teachers, log-linear model tests were used. The results of these tests showed statistically significant differences between the teachers, with regard to 'content' as well as 'behaviour' ($p < .05$). The dimension 'content' turned out to be more sensitive to teacher effects than the dimension 'behaviour'. Literary-history teachers, for instance, elicited significantly more statements of students in the content categories 'literary contextual information' and 'non-literary contextual information', whereas the students of text-experiencing teachers reported more learning experiences with regard to 'specific works of fiction' and the 'relationship literary text/reader'. Apparently, there are effects of 'teacher' on what students say they have learned from literature lessons. The size and the consistency of the teacher-effects substantiate the validity of the learner report.

Chantal and Alex: Two Approaches to Teaching Literature

The results of this study encouraged us to explore further the learning experiences of students by way of learner reports. We especially wanted to know more about the relationship between the educational practice of teachers and the ensuing learning outcomes, as reported by students. To what extent can differences in learning outcomes be explained by features of the educational practice?

In our second study two teachers of Dutch collaborated: 'Chantal' and 'Alex'. These teachers were chosen because of their differences in opinion and self-reported practice of literature teaching. The teachers were chosen out of 600 teachers who filled in a written questionnaire and out of twelve teachers who gave an interview about the content and methods of their literature teaching. Chantal and Alex both seemed to be representative of a large group of teachers (Janssen and Rijlaarsdam, 1995; Janssen, 1994).

The educational practice of these teachers, as reported in the written questionnaire and in the interviews, can be described in brief as follows.

Chantal is a representative of a cognitive, literary-history approach to teaching literature. Her main goal is to transmit knowledge of the cultural heritage. The subject-matter she teaches is focussed on literary history, historical literature, stylistics and poetics. In her literature classes she discusses (fragments of) Dutch literary classics. Before reading a text with the students, she gives them extensive information about the life and times of the author, the literary movement to which the author belongs, his/her work, main themes, style of writing, etc. Students have to learn the main points of this information by heart. Then, representative fragments are read and examined. The direction and content of that examination is in the teacher's control. She interprets the text for the students. Chantal's teaching method is characterized by teacher-dominated whole-class instruction. The emphasis is on lecturing, telling and reading aloud; students listen and take notes. Occasionally students have to write a paper or give a lecture on a literary subject, but on the whole receptive activities (listening and reading) predominate.

Alex, on the other hand, emphasizes the personal development of students as the main goal of his literature teaching. He sets great store by affective aspects of reading fiction; learning to appreciate fiction, being able to identify oneself with characters in a story, bringing one's own personal experiences into it, in order to make sense of a text. He teaches little or no literary history. Central to his teaching are: reading fiction and talking about it. The very use of the term 'fiction', instead of 'literature', is indicative of Alex's opinion of the texts to be discussed. The texts Alex discusses in the classroom are predominantly modern short stories, classics as well as less known stories, but he also discusses film and video. Starting points of the classroom discussions are the personal responses of the students. By talking about literature, Alex wants to confront his students with different interpretations of the same text and to show them that the way in which a text is interpreted by readers is linked to their personal experiences in the outside world. In addition to classroom discussions, Alex occasionally uses teamwork as a teaching method, working with small groups of students.

To collect more factual information about the literature teaching of the teachers, we observed and tape-recorded about ten literature lessons of each teacher. We focussed on an important didactic device teachers frequently use, irrespective of the content and method of their teaching: asking questions.[6] All questions Chantal and Alex asked concerning literature were analyzed. The analysis revealed strong differences in the type of questions they asked their students. Six main differences were found:

(i) Chantal asked more 'reproductive' questions, requiring students to recognize or remember certain earlier acquired factual, declarative knowledge, than Alex (63 per cent of Chantal's questions versus 24 per cent of Alex's questions).

Alex's questions appealed less often to memory and more often to 'productive' activities, requiring students to generate 'new' information, by reasoning, creative or critical thinking (68 versus 29 per cent).

(ii) About half of the questions Chantal asked were questions about the subject-matter she wanted to transmit, in particular historical, literary and non-literary contextual information (49 per cent).

These kind of questions were lacking in Alex's lessons. He asked predominantly 'textual' questions, questions concerning (the contents or form of) a specific literary text read by the students (93 per cent).

(iii) The textual questions of Alex for the most part referred to modern short stories, Chantal's textual questions for the most part referred to poems.

(iv) Alex asked more interpretative questions about literary texts, requiring students to infer meanings, than Chantal (18 versus 6 per cent of the textual questions).

(v) Alex appealed more often to a personal, individual handling of the literary text, requiring students to point out their problems, elaborate on the text or reflect on their reading processes (15 versus 0 per cent of the textual questions). Also, Alex asked students more often for an evaluative or emotive response to literary texts (25 versus 1 per cent of the textual questions).

The nature of Chantal's questions was more often impersonal or neutral, asking students to read a text aloud or to identify the period, author, genre or to identify stylistic or structural means used by the author (47 versus 4 per cent of the textual questions).

(vi) Alex, more often than Chantal, asked questions in the area of intertextuality, requiring students to form bridges between the literary text and other literary texts they had read previously (18 versus 12 per cent of the textual questions).

The differences in the questions the teachers ask point in the direction one might have expected. Chantal's literary historical approach goes together with reproductive, non-textual questions, particularly in the area of (literary) contextual information. Alex's 'personal development' approach goes together with personal questions, encouraging students to produce evaluative and interpretative responses to literary texts.

Expected Differences in Learning Outcomes

Considering the differences between Chantal's and Alex's literature teaching, especially the differences in the repertoire of questions they ask their students, it is likely that there are also differences in perceived benefits. The students of Chantal will probably report differing learning experiences than the students of Alex.

We formulated the following hypotheses concerning the learning experiences of their students:

(a) Significantly more students of Chantal will make statements about factual, declarative knowledge they acquired, in particular knowledge about literary and non-literary history (see above: differences (i) and (ii)).

(b) Significantly more students of Alex will refer to what they have learned about reading and interpreting (specific) literary texts (see above: (ii) and (iv)).

(c) Significantly more students of Alex will make statements about prose, while Chantal's students will make statements about poetry (see above: (iii)).

(d) Significantly more students of Alex will make personal, affective statements: statements about themselves, about the self-knowledge they acquired, their attitudes or feelings towards literature or about the effects or functions of literature. Chantal's students are more likely to report 'impersonal' or neutral learning experiences, concerning literature or 'the world' in general (see above: (v)).

(e) Significantly more students of Alex will refer to knowledge and skills in the area of intertextuality (see above: (vi)).

Actual Learning Outcomes

To test our hypotheses we asked students of Chantal and Alex to write a learner report.[7] Per teacher two classes of 16–18-year-olds participated: the final grade of general secondary education (havo) and the last grade but one of pre-university education (vwo). We collected ninety-one reports: forty by students of Chantal, fifty-one by students of Alex. Their answers on the multiple choice questions in the reports showed that the two groups of students were comparable in other respects than average age and grade. No statistically significant differences were found in gender, interest in literature in general or frequency of reading for pleasure between the two groups. Nor did we find a difference in familiarity with the task of writing a learner report: most students of both groups were unfamiliar with the task.

The reports contained 682 statements about the benefits of literature teaching. Chantal's students tended to report more learning experiences (an average of nine statements per student) than Alex's students (an average of six statements per student).

Each single statement was analyzed, using an improved version of our classification system. Per teacher, *the proportion of students* who produced

Table 5.1: Chantal: top-five learning experiences mentioned by most students (in percentages of students)

Category of learning experiences	% students
1 Positive attitude towards literary texts	80
For example I have discovered that I like reading books	
2 Declarative knowledge concerning literary history	55
For example I have discovered that Dutch literature is older than I always supposed	
3 Negative attitude towards literary texts	45
For example I have noticed that I hate poetry	
4 Metacognitive knowledge concerning learning/studying	40
For example I have learned that it's better to do my homework regularly, for then I remember more and I obtain higher marks	
5 Positive attitude towards literature teaching	33
For example I have learned that Mrs C. teaches literature well: I always listen to her	

one or more statements in each cell of the classification system was determined. We preferred 'proportion of students' to 'proportion of statements' in our analysis, in order to avoid the possibility that only one or two idiosyncratic students (students who produce a lot of statements in one cell of our classification scheme) would be responsible for significant differences between the two groups as a whole.

Results

To give the reader an impression of what kind of learning experiences the students reported, we present two top-five lists of statements; one top-five for the students of Chantal (table 5.1) and one for the students of Alex (table 5.2).

The tables show that both groups of students most often express a positive attitude towards specific literary texts, literature or reading in general: 80 per cent of Chantal's students and 51 per cent of Alex's students make one or more statements that fall into this category. In both groups there are also students who express a negative attitude towards literature: 45 per cent of Chantal's and 27 per cent of Alex's group indicate that they have discovered they dislike all (or some) literature.

From these findings it can be deduced that some students express a positive attitude and a negative attitude simultaneously. This can be accounted for by statements about developments in literary taste. Students of both teachers report having discovered liking certain kinds of books, authors or genres, while disliking other genres.

In all other respects the two top-five lists differ remarkably. Chantal's students most often indicate they have learned something about literary history, how to study and perform well at school, or about literature teaching in general.

Table 5.2: Alex: top-five learning experiences mentioned by most students
(in percentages of students)

Category of learning experiences	% students
1 Positive attitude towards literary texts	51
For example I have learned that I like reading a lot	
2 Declarative knowledge concerning interpretation	45
For example I have discovered that a lot of things in books have a double meaning	
3 Metacognitive knowledge concerning interpretation	31
For example I have learned that I am not able to grasp the deeper meaning of literary books	
4 Declarative knowledge concerning relationship text/reader	29
For example I know now that reading books can sometimes help me to forget my worries	
5 Negative attitude towards literary texts	27
For example I have discovered that I fervently dislike literature	
Metacognitive knowledge concerning literary texts	27
For example I have learned that I have difficulties in reading a book well	

Alex's students, on the other hand, indicate that they have learned about (the problems of) literary interpretation and about the relationship between text and reader.

There seems to be evidence, then, that the students of Chantal and Alex vary in what they have learned from literature lessons. But to what extent do the differences support our hypotheses?

In order to test our hypotheses, a chi-square-test was performed for each of the cells of the classification scheme. The results of these tests showed statistically significant differences ($p < .05$) between the two groups of students.

For each of the significant differences in proportion the effect size index (h) was calculated. Effect-size is an aid for assessing the practical significance of group differences (Cohen, 1988). According to Cohen, an effect-size equal to or larger than .80 is a large effect. An effect-size smaller than .80, but larger than or equal to .50 is considered to be an effect of medium size. An effect-size smaller than .50 is considered to be a small effect.

In table 5.3 the significant differences in learning experiences are presented, along with their effect sizes.

Firstly, table 5.3 shows that significantly more students of Chantal make statements that fall into the category 'declarative knowledge concerning literary history' than students of Alex. This effect is, in terms of Cohen, a large effect. There is also a significant difference in the amount of 'declarative knowledge concerning non-literary backgrounds'. This effect is of a medium size. These findings support our first hypothesis, according to which more students of Chantal (than of Alex) make statements about factual, declarative knowledge they acquired, in particular knowledge about literary and non-literary history.

Secondly, table 5.3 shows that significantly more students of Alex report

Table 5.3: Significant differences in learning experiences between Chantal's and Alex's students: size and observed direction of differences
h = index for differences between proportions;
ES = effect size (small: h = .20, medium: h = .50, large: h = .80).
direction: C > A = more often reported by Chantal's students;
             A > C = more often reported by Alex's students;
             * = in line with hypothesis

Category of learning experiences	h	ES	direction
Declarative knowledge concerning literary history	1.20	large	C > A*
Declarative knowledge concerning non-literary backgrounds	.60	medium	C > A*
Declarative knowledge concerning interpretation	.80	large	A > C*
Metacognitive knowledge concerning interpretation	.70	medium	A > C*
Declarative knowledge concerning poetry-analysis	.40	small	C > A*
Declarative knowledge concerning relationship text/reader	.70	medium	A > C*
Declarative knowledge concerning intertextuality	.30	small	A > C*
Positive attitude towards literature teaching	.80	large	C > A
Positive attitude towards literary texts	.70	medium	C > A
Positive attitude towards compulsory reading	.30	small	C > A
Metacognitive knowledge concerning learning/studying	.80	large	C > A

about (declarative and metacognitive) knowledge concerning the processes or results of literary interpretation. For instance, they say (more often than Chantal's students) that literary texts are liable to more than one interpretation and that they have discovered themselves to be good or bad at interpreting literature. These differences are of large or medium size.

These findings also seem to point in the hypothesized direction, for our second hypothesis assumed that more of Alex's students would make statements concerning reading and interpreting (specific) literary texts.

Thirdly, table 5.3 indicates that more students of Chantal tend to have learned something about the analysis of poetry than students of Alex. They report declarative knowledge: having learned that poems are built in such-and-such a way. The effect is small, and only partly supports our third hypothesis, according to which more of Chantal's students would make statements about poetry, while more of Alex's students would report on prose. This last effect was not found.

Fourthly, table 5.3 shows that more students of Alex make one or more statements about what they have learned concerning the relationship between text and reader than Chantal's students. They, for instance, remark on what a literary text can do to a reader (emotional effects of reading) or on the function of reading. The difference is of a medium size. This finding is in line with part of our fourth hypothesis. However, the effect that Alex's students would be more 'personal' across the board, while Chantal's students would make more 'impersonal' statements, was not found.

Fifthly, table 5.3 shows that more of Alex's students make statements about their acquired knowledge of intertextuality than Chantal's students. Alex's students, for instance, report that they have learned that there are connections between literary texts or that literary texts may refer to other literary texts. The effect is small. According to our fifth hypothesis, more of Alex's students would refer to their knowledge and skills in the area of intertextuality. This hypothesis is partly confirmed, namely the knowledge-part.

Lastly, table 5.3 also shows differences between the groups of students that were *not* predicted. More of Chantal's students refer to positive attitudes they acquired as a result of the literature lessons: positive attitudes towards literary texts, compulsory reading or the literature lessons in general. They also say (more often than Alex's students) they have learned about their own achievements at school, in particular in the subject-area of literature, or about good and bad ways to study the subject-matter or learn it by heart. These kinds of remarks are significantly less often made by Alex's students. These unpredicted differences are for the most part medium sized.

All in all, our assumptions with regard to students' learning experiences proved to be partly true. We found that the learning experiences of the students of Chantal and Alex did differ significantly and that most of the differences pointed in the direction we anticipated (and formulated in five hypotheses).

However, one of our five hypotheses was not substantiated. Alex's affective approach to teaching literature did *not* elicit more affective or personal learning experiences than Chantal's cognitive approach. Thus it is not the case that Alex's students score higher on reading enjoyment than Chantal's students. On the contrary. More students of Chantal expressed positive feelings or attitudes towards specific literary texts or literature in general than did Alex's students. They also expressed more often a positive attitude towards literature teaching than did the students of Alex.

Summary and Discussion

The findings of our research indicate that 16–18-year-old students are indeed able to write down what they have learned from literature lessons in a learner report. We also found evidence that this kind of self-assessment can be a valid instrument for tracing effects of literary education. The learner report proved to be sensitive enough to reveal differences in perceived benefits from different forms of literature teaching.

Results of a survey showed that in the educational practice of teachers there are at least two conceptions of literature as a school subject: literature viewed as promoting 'cultural literacy' and literature viewed as promoting 'personal development' of students. In the present study we found indications that these two conceptions culminate in very different learning experiences of students, not only in theory but also in practice. A 'cultural literacy' approach tends to elicit above all factual or declarative knowledge concerning literary history, non-literary backgrounds of literature and poetry-analysis. A 'personal development' approach, on the other hand, tends to elicit declarative and metacognitive knowledge concerning the interpretation of literary texts, the phenomenon of intertextuality and concerning the relationship between literary text and reader. These are statistically significant differences in learning outcomes, confirming our assumptions. Contrary to expectations, we found no evidence that a more affective, 'personal development' approach towards literature teaching culminates in more affective or personal learning experiences or that it leads to more reading enjoyment of students than a more cognitive 'cultural literacy' approach. We found just the opposite.

There are several limitations and possible objections to the present study. In the first place, only a small number of teachers was involved: one 'cultural literacy'-teacher and one 'personal development'-teacher. Should we not rather speak of (individual) teacher effects, instead of approach effects?

However, the teachers involved were not randomly selected. They were carefully chosen out of a cross-section of teachers who participated in a national survey. Both Chantal and Alex are in many respects 'prototypes': in their goals, but also with respect to the content and form of their literature teaching. This means that we may, to a certain extent, generalize our findings. Although obviously all teachers have their own 'personal touch' and not all cultural-literacy teachers or all personal-development teachers are alike, many more similarities are to be found *within* both groups of teachers than *between* the two groups.

Secondly, in our analysis of the learner reports we distinguished different categories of learning experiences of students. With regard to declarative knowledge concerning literary history, non-literary backgrounds, interpretation, poetry-analysis, relationship text/reader, intertextuality and with regard to metacognitive knowledge concerning interpretation, significant differences were found in the hypothesized direction (see table 5.3). The question arises if these variables are really independent of each other, or if there are other underlying dimensions. If the variables proved to be highly correlated, this would invalidate the outcomes of our study.

Correlations were calculated between the seven mentioned variables. In only two out of the forty-two cases significant positive correlations were found between variables. These correlations were relatively low (.30). Apparently, dependencies did not play a large part in our analysis.

Thirdly, our strictly quantitative approach has limitations in itself. Learning outcomes are presented in terms of proportions of students making one or more statements that fall in the same category of learning experiences. The quality of their statements was not taken into account. Therefore, it is possible that the learning outcomes of one group of students may have more 'depth' or are more differentiated than the learning outcomes of another group of students, although no differences were found in proportion of students or proportion of statements. Further research along these lines is necessary and possible.

Also, it should be noted that we considered in our present study only *short term* effects of literature teaching. One may assume that differences in learning effects will 'fade out' in time. It is fruitful to ask former students what they still remember of the literature lessons at school and what they have learned from those lessons, in order to reveal long-term effects. Therefore, we approached ex-students of Chantal and Alex and asked them to write a learner report as well. Results of this study will be published shortly.

Finally, the main assumption underlying our study, that there is a direct relationship between educational practice and results (different practices lead to different results) may be criticized. This assumption reflects a rather conservative, 'input–output' view of the processes of teaching and learning. These processes are more complex and determined by more parameters than is suggested in this chapter. It also should be noted that the same results can be achieved by very different approaches.

Moreover, in analyzing the 'input' we focussed on just one didactic device (i.e. the questions teachers ask their students), while the 'output' or results of literature teaching were measured in an indirect way: by way of self-assessments instead of by way of some kind of 'objective' literary knowledge and comprehension test.

If no differences in learning experiences had been found all this would present a severe drawback. As it is, the study provides support for the idea that there are large differences in learning outcomes between different approaches towards literature teaching. In spite of the limitations of our methods, four out of five hypotheses concerning differences in learning outcomes were confirmed, and some of these differences were (in terms of Cohen's effect size) very large indeed. In other words, the results of the study seem to legitimize the methods we used.

Nevertheless, it is important to note the exploratory nature of our study. Why, for example, our findings concerning affective or personal learning experiences were the other way around (the cognitive approach of Chantal resulting in more personal and more positive learning outcomes than the affective approach of Alex) remains unexplained. One possible explanation is that other, unexamined features of their literature teaching play a part. Chantal, for one, devotes more time to teaching literature than Alex. Furthermore, she tends to read many literary texts in the classroom, without further questioning them, while Alex tends to examine a few texts thoroughly. Maybe an extensive approach (such as Chantal's) is more conducive to a positive attitude towards reading literature than an intensive approach (such as Alex's).

It is also possible that part of the students' responses may be due to their backgrounds and/or to social desirability effects. Chantal's students, for instance, are predominantly from a Protestant background, contrary to Alex's students, who are probably in the majority not religiously orientated. Maybe 'religion' and other background-variables are related to 'reading interest', 'reading enjoyment' or 'personal involvement in reading literature'. (The results of our multiple choice questions, however, do not point in that direction: no significant differences in interest in literature or frequency of reading for pleasure between Chantal's and Alex's students were found.) All in all, the present study does not disclose what precisely causes the differences in students' affective responses to literature reading and teaching.

Notes

1   In the Netherlands, literature is part of the curriculum in the fourth, fifth and sixth years of general secondary school, when students are 15–18-years-old. In the Dutch education system general secondary education is divided into pre-university education (vwo) and senior general secondary education (havo). Pre-university education lasts six years and prepares students for university training. Senior general secondary education lasts five years and prepares students for higher vocational training.

2   The new programme for the second phase of general secondary education (education of 15–18-year-olds) will be implemented in 1998.

3   The study is part of a research programme of the Graduate School of Teaching and Learning of the University of Amsterdam, entitled 'The Teaching and Learning of Cognitive Strategies'.

4   This study is reported on in detail by Janssen and Rijlaarsdam (1990a, 1990b and 1992). See also Rijlaarsdam and Janssen, chapter 4 in this volume.

5   The distinction between a 'text studying' and a 'text experiencing' approach to learning to read fiction and non-fiction derives from Ten Brinke (1976) p. 86.

6   We use the notion 'question' in a wide sense: every utterance that requires a response of students, in some form or other. A more detailed report of this study is in preparation (Janssen, 1995).

7   Half of the students of each teacher received version A of the report, starting with 'Rules concerning the world', the other half received version B, starting with 'Rules concerning oneself'. Analysis of variance showed that there was indeed an effect of 'version': students produced significantly more statements in the first section of the learner report than in the following sections (version A: $F (1, 89) = 11.88$, $p < .001$ and version B: $F (1, 89) = 7.94$, $p < .01$). By using two, randomly distributed versions this effect is (partly) eliminated.

References

COHEN, J. (1988) *Statistical Power Analysis for the Behavioral Sciences*, (2nd ed.), Hillsdale, NJ, Lawrence Erlbaum Associates.

DE GROOT, A.D. (1978) 'Wat neemt de leerling mee van onderwijs? Gedragsrepertoires, programma's, kennis-en-vaardigheden' ('What do students take with them from education? Behavioral repertoires, programmes, knowledge-and-skills'), *Handboek onderwijspraktijk*, afl. 2, januari.

DE GROOT, A.D. (1980) 'Over leerervaringen en leerdoelen' ('About learning experiences and objectives'), *Handboek onderwijspraktijk*, afl. 10, november.

EISNER, E.W. (1969) 'Instructional and expressive educational objectives: their formulation and use in curriculum' in POPHAM, W.J.E., EISNER, E.W., SULLIVAN, H.J. and TYLER, L.L. (Eds) *Instructional Objectives*, Chicago, IL, Rand McNally.

JANSSEN, T. (1994) 'Verscheidenheid in eenheid en eenheid in verscheidenheid. Twaalf docenten Nederlands over hun literatuuronderwijs in de bovenbouw van havo en vwo' ('Unity and diversity: Twelve teachers of Dutch literature about their educational practice in the final grades of secondary schools'), *Spiegel*, **12**, 3, pp. 7–43.

JANSSEN, T. (1995) 'Zijn er nog problemen? Docentvragen en tekstverwerkingsactiviteiten in literatuurlessen Nederlands' ('Are there still any problems? Teacher questions and text processing activities in the literature classroom'), paper ten behoeve van de conferentie 'Literatuuronderwijs: relaties van onderzoek en onderwijs, Zeist, oktober.

JANSSEN, T. and RIJLAARSDAM, G. (1990a) 'What do students learn from literature teaching?' in HAYHOE, M. and PARKER, S. (Eds) *Reading and Response*, Buckingham, Open University Press, pp. 94–106.

JANSSEN, T. and RIJLAARSDAM, G. (1990b) 'Opbrengsten van literatuuronderwijs: een vooronderzoek' ('Results of literature teaching: a pilot study'), *Spiegel*, **8**, 2, pp. 29–47.

JANSSEN, T. and RIJLAARSDAM, G. (1992) 'Het learner report in de praktijk van de bovenbouw' ('Learning Reports in Teaching Practices in Higher Secondary Education') in MOOR, W. DE and VAN WOERKOM, M. (Eds) *Literaire Competentie, Het doel van Literatuuronderwijs*, Den Haag, NBLC, pp. 209–22.

JANSSEN, T. and RIJLAARSDAM, G. (1995) 'Approaches to the teaching of literature. A survey of literary education in secondary schools in the Netherlands' in KREUZ, R.J. and MACNEALY, M.S. (Eds) *Empirical Approaches to Literature and Aesthetics*, Norwood, NJ, Ablex Publishing Corporation.

PURVES, A.C. (1971) 'Evaluation of learning in literature' in BLOOM, B.S., HASTINGS, J.T. and MADAUS, G.F. (Eds) *Handbook on Formative and Summative Evaluation of Student Learning*, New York, McGraw-Hill Book Company.

TEN BRINKE, S. (1976) *The Complete Mother-tongue Curriculum*, Groningen, Wolters-Noordhoff-Longman.

VAN DER KAMP, M. (1980) *Wat neemt de leerling mee van kunstzinnige vorming?* (What does a student learn from art education?) 's-Gravenhage, Stichting voor Onderzoek van het Onderwijs, SVO-reeks 29.

VAN KESTEREN, B.J. (1989) 'Gebruiksmogelijkheden van het learner report' ('Possibilities to use the learner report'), *Tijdschrift voor Onderwijsresearch*, **14**, 1, pp. 13–29.

WITTE, T. (1995) 'Van de nood een deugd. Perspectieven voor vakoverstijgend literatuuronderwijs in de tweede fase' ('Perspectives for extra-curricular literature teaching'), *Levende Talen*, **499**, pp. 191–9.

6 Outside Forster's Machine: Re-representing Technology in the Age of Cyberspace

Neil Campbell

Anybody in our culture is regarded as invited as long as he stays in one fixed position. Once he starts moving around and crossing boundaries, he's delinquent, he's fair game. (McLuhan in Stearn, 1968, p. 13)

Pupils should be given opportunities, where appropriate, to develop and apply their information technology (IT) capability in their study of English. (National Curriculum, English Common Requirements, 1995, p. 1)

Culture is not seen as monolithic or unchanging, but as a site of multiple and heterogeneous borders where different histories, languages, experiences, and voices intermingle amidst diverse relations of power and privilege. (Giroux in Grossberg *et al.*, 1992, p. 205)

Everybody in authority seemed to want us to stay in one place. (bell hooks, 1994, p. 3)

This chapter proposes and plays with approaches to cultural texts in ways that will be both familiar and unfamiliar to readers and is based upon a number of convictions about the way we teach and the way students learn.[1] It begins in the personal but has an underlying political purpose, which is to explore the need for greater flexibility and trust in the teaching of 'literacy' at all levels of the education system. In particular, I am using the focus of media technologies as a means of addressing questions of approaches to teaching and learning that restate the need for interdisciplinary or transdisciplinary study, for a general suspicion of fixed educational boundaries, and for a recognition of the complex debates about technoculture and how these might be productively used in teaching. In examining the machine, we confront questions about our own changing roles, identity, gender and our relations to power and control. This, therefore, is a chapter of boundary-crossings, as McLuhan and Giroux put it, of adventures in the new spaces that can be created by interdisciplinary or transdisciplinary studies, the terrain of the 'cyborg' that 'acknowledges the interdependence of people and things, and just how blurry the boundaries between them have become' (Leigh Star, 1995, p. 21). Following the theories of Donna Haraway, I will suggest that technology should be integral to any reconsideration of literacy in the future and should permeate teaching as it does everyday life, and in particular the life of the young. As Haraway (1991) writes, a 'cyborg' culture 'is about transgressed boundaries, potent fusions, and dangerous possibilities which progressive people might explore as one part of needed political work' (p. 154). I believe teachers at all levels, along with their students, can be these 'progressive people' contesting the meanings and uses of technology in a complex society which traditionally divides human and machine over issues of control, in order to imagine and explore a social order in which 'people are not afraid of their joint kinship with animals and machines, not afraid of partial identities and contradictory standpoints' (*ibid.*). At the centre, for Haraway and for my argument, is the fear of a 'single vision' (*ibid.*), what I will term a 'monologic', single-disciplined view of things, for it 'produces worse illusions' (*ibid.*) and imposes itself as 'the one code that translates all meaning perfectly' (*ibid.*, p. 176). In our relations with technology, we are made aware of multiple differences that move away from simple divisions like mind-body, male-female, whole-part, child-adult and so on, and enter a world in which 'we find ourselves to be cyborgs, hybrids, mosaics, chimeras' (*ibid.*, p. 177). Through this process, we might begin to understand identity as something unfixed, in process, and constantly being reformed and constructed by a variety of cultural discourses, of which technology is of central importance.

EM Forster's *The Machine Stops* (1909)

I begin in my own experience, as student and teacher, working with a much-used short story *The Machine Stops* by EM Forster. Its view of technology is usually read as dystopian, an answer to the utopian explorations of HG Wells, but its effects are conservative, for they emphasize a certain view of humanity mistrusting technology and therefore trapped by it. 'I want to see you not through the machine', cries Kuno, the story's protagonist (Forster in Barnes and Egford, 1973, p. 127). The Machine rules and controls by transmission of selected information and excludes 'nuances of expression' (*ibid.*, p. 129) and rejects the complex and contradictory 'imponderable bloom' of things in preference for the 'general idea'. The story is concerned with the possibility of intervening in this technological processing of the human to rediscover the elements of humanity that include such complexities and imponderables. This desire is a desire for earth, but is 'contrary to the spirit of the age . . . contrary to the Machine' (*ibid.*, p. 130), which has become dominant and encapsulated people away from the climates of the earth, giving instead a room 'like the cell of a bee' in which all needs are catered for in a 'delirium of acquiescence' (*ibid.*, p. 132). Homogeneity is the characteristic of the Machine-world, with all 'exactly the same' (*ibid.*, p. 142), and having created it, humans are 'robbed ... of the sense of space and of the sense of touch, (for the Machine) ... has blurred every human relation and narrowed down love to a carnal act ...' (*ibid.*, pp. 150–1). In Kuno's dark, dystopian vision, 'we only exist as the blood corpuscles that course through its arteries, and if it could work without us, it would let us die' (*ibid.*, p. 151). As the story ends, with the Machine stopping, the dependent people die, 'strangled in the garments that they had woven' (*ibid.*, p. 166), but they 'have recaptured life' beyond the confines of the Machine. As they die, victims of the technology they created, the story tells of others, the 'Homeless' who have survived outside the Machine and live as real humans on the margins of the closed world. In them, the story suggests, is the future, the glimpse of 'the untainted sky' (*ibid.*, p. 167).

The story, much used in schools, demonstrates a view of technology rooted in its age — the early 1900s — but also reflecting subsequent concerns about technology and society. It divides the positions very starkly in order to make its point about the loss of human values in the rush to technological development. The Machine is bad here. It destroys and transforms human beings into the 'white pap' of conformity and the only salvation lies *outside the Machine* amid the vagaries of nature. Reading this story again for the first time in fifteen or more years, I am struck by its technophobia, its linking of the machine with a hopeless lack of control and with destructive, unforgiving nihilism. All the potential benefits of machines are reduced to a narrow ideological myth, as Roland Barthes would term it, in which other meanings are diminished or erased from consideration. Myth, writes Barthes,

> abolishes the complexity of human acts, it gives them the simplicity of essences, *it does away with all dialectics*, with any going back beyond what is immediately visible, *it organizes a world that is without contradictions* ... it establishes a blissful clarity. (Barthes, 1976, p. 143 — my emphasis)

Ironically, the characteristics that Forster gives the Machine are also true for his narrative, which limits and closes our views on technology and replaces the possible contradictions with a controlled discourse; it is 'mythical speech'. However, as Barthes writes, this is not simply a written form, for it is carried in all 'representations' (*ibid.*, p. 110) across a range of disciplines.

My contention here is that to examine a text like Forster's is to almost certainly follow the logic of his myth of technology and to reinforce the particular arguments that the story generates about values and ideology. It is important, therefore, to spread wider in the exploration of representations in order to extend Forster's monological approach into a dialogue within which different notions of technology are in contest. As Barthes writes, in myths like Forster's, 'the meaning is *already* complete, it postulates a kind of knowledge, a past, a memory, a comparative order of facts, ideas, decisions' (*ibid.*, p. 117). Thus whilst vilifying technology, the story celebrates the individual (Kuno's efforts to escape), the family and the resilience of the human spirit — all tenets of the social order one might define as conventional and hegemonic.

At the very end of the story, through the figures of the 'Homeless', there exists a means of opposing the dominant reading of the story, for they represent those outside the conservative mainstream values, who have nonetheless found ways of surviving the Machine. Donna Haraway (1991) calls upon outsiders (in her argument, feminists, women of colour, etc.), 'the bastard race', who will teach us about 'the power of the margins' (p. 176) to raise questions and debate them with the 'informatics of domination' (*ibid.*, p. 181). Forster's 'Homeless' are those who have no home in this story or cannot locate themselves inside the neat, curtailed world of this myth of technology. Students reading this story today may recognize the possibility that technology has contributed to and altered lives in ways other than the negative and feel themselves to be 'homeless' in the narrative. In fact, students would be more likely to feel 'at home' in the Machine than outside it and so to exclude them and to deny their experience is to continue and perpetuate the narrowing of focus in teaching. To read the story only from within the myth of technology as bad will reduce the text and alienate the readers, but to offer different approaches and combinations with other texts may generate dialogues on the subjects of identity, power, and gender in relation to the specific representations of technology in our age. The voices of the 'Homeless' open up the text and challenge the closed and limited readings of the traditional text. Too often in the classroom, the students are the homeless, pushed to the margins and excluded from the centrally-determined authoritarian definition of what is acceptable and why.

Beyond *The Machine Stops*, or alongside it, one would wish to 'read' other texts or representations of technology; films, video games, comics, computer technologies, as well as new science fiction. Forster's Machine is like a stifling curriculum, hemmed in by narrow objectives, learning outcomes and single disciplinary approaches, all conspiring to close down the imaginative engagement of the student in a dialogical relationship with a variety of materials. 'We require regeneration, not rebirth' argues Haraway (*ibid.*, p. 181), and one means of regenerating the curriculum is through imaginative interconnections of different texts, learning from the cultural studies movement that texts must be questioned, problematized and seen as revealing complex relations of power, ideology and dominance, as well as pleasure and empowerment.[2]

Finding a Home for the 'Homeless': Interdisciplinary Studies

Throughout the 1970s there was an important struggle to gain credibility for media and film studies in secondary schools and central to it was the belief that interdisciplinary study might help break away from 'the fragmentation of knowledge into a set of discrete subjects which have an imaginary unity in the hierarchy of the curriculum rather than the unity of knowledge in its production in social practices' (Donald, 1980, p. 3). Rather than create such boundaries, media studies wished to emphasize how meanings were constructed and reproduced, drawing attention to wider political and ideological issues that were contained within this process. The National Curriculum's suspicion of media studies is evident, consigning it to 'English' and so placing it firmly back into its former home and denying a significant place for a crucial area of youth experience and understanding.

In my darkest thoughts, I suspect this is the very reason. The demand to impose learning extends to a fear of utilizing a point of access that the students themselves find pleasurable, interesting and stimulating. Computer technology, of various levels of sophistication, is familiar territory for the majority of young people and they are actively engaged in a dialogue with its various possibilities. Again a contemporary myth of technology, following on from Forster's Machine, would have us believe that video games and computer software have reduced the young to passive receivers of images and ideas, when in fact the opposite is just as likely to be true — that the machine has empowered, has provided a point of contact, a means of expression that is used actively and creatively. Regardless of this particular argument, and whether we approve or disapprove of new technologies, they exist and are a major part of people's lives. For education, at all levels, to ignore its potential seems self-defeating and narrow-sighted, for it defines 'literacy' in a very limited manner. The privileging of certain types of written literature; the 'recommended books' of the National Curriculum and the set texts at 'A' level and at university, if seen as exclusive and important modes of expression in our culture, perpetuate a hegemonic structure contrary to the lived experience of most of us. We, as teachers at all levels, must be aware of our part in that hegemony and a significant element in our thinking about future literacy and teaching must be to 'consider the different ways people participate in social, cultural, economic, and political life' and acknowledge 'not only that these are related but that they are themselves the sites of struggle', and that as educators, through our various practices 'hegemony is constructed' (Grossberg in Giroux and McLaren, 1994, p. 21). Reminding ourselves of this may permit reconsiderations and questionings of what we teach, how we teach it and how it is received, but also provide the occasion to rethink how we might revalue what lies beyond our own educational boundaries. Across the border are techniques in practice that can be appropriated and used productively to raise significant new questions.

Traditional literary studies, as advanced in institutional frameworks of power, are only ever a fraction of the communications that exist around us in our lives and the curriculum must reflect this multifaceted culture. Peim (1993) suggests that

> productive effects might be achieved by looking at texts of disparate kinds and by looking at cultural phenomena that are not usually defined as texts (in order to) . . . move away from the idea that 'reading' itself is identical with literature, or . . . 'the literary text'. (p. 103)

The single discipline approach seems increasingly restrictive in the readings proposed by Peim, for our lives involve a more complex intertextual experience wherein image, sound, graphic and written forms continually interweave to form the environments of the everyday. To then reflect upon that experience with reference to one specific mode of expression does appear counter-productive as education.

In Michel Foucault's theories, the term 'discipline' takes on a particular set of meanings as 'general formulas of domination' (Rabinow, 1986, p. 181), 'a machinery of power that explores it (the body), breaks it down and rearranges it' and 'produces subjected and practiced bodies, "docile" bodies . . .' (*ibid.*, p. 182). He goes on to add that 'the nature of the Norm appears through the disciplines . . . established as a principle of coercion in teaching with the introduction of a standardized education . . .' and the end product is 'homogeneity' (*ibid.*, p. 196). One can see this in the narrow definition of literacy, the insistence upon canonical texts and the marginalization of alternative modes of expression. Foucault wrote that 'education may well be . . . the instrument whereby every individual . . . can gain access to any kind of discourse. But we know that in its distribution, in what it permits and prevents, it follows the well-trodden battle lines of social conflict' (Foucault, 1972, p. 227).

Single disciplines tend to delimit and foreclose the meanings and cross-references between different types of texts, because of the structured approach that only asks certain questions in certain ways. The need for a dialogical approach may be more relevant than ever as an effort to guard against assumptions of fixed meanings, closed texts and unitary language. Poststructuralism has demonstrated that texts are polysemic, contain many meanings, and that to reduce them and exclude the overspill of readings is to deny the voices generated by and through any text. As Mikhail Bakhtin recognized, there are many voices running through literature, as in culture itself, and these must be acknowledged in an ideally 'heteroglossic' formulation of society:

> at any given moment of its historical existence, language is heteroglot
> from top to bottom: it represents the co-existence of socio-ideological
> contradictions between the present and the past . . . these 'languages'
> of heteroglossia intersect each other in a variety of ways, forming new
> socially typifying 'languages'. (Bakhtin, 1990, p. 291)

This dynamic view of ever-changing languages of culture is vital to a forward-looking curriculum that has the courage to follow the intersecting lines of such social genres and hybrid forms. To cling only to a predefined sense of the past runs the risk of alienating the progressive realities of a fluid culture which in part includes 'a heteroglossia consciously opposed to this literary language' of the mainstream, and indeed 'aimed sharply and polemically against the official languages of its given time' (*ibid.*, p. 273). If educational practice becomes monologic, that is centred around a limited single-voice that casts itself as the

determinant voice of the offical culture, then it perpetuates a system of aliena-
tion and disempowerment that may push students' experience to the edges of
the academic arena. This is my sense of the National Curriculum as a potential
legitimator of established canons, predefined (by whom?) as 'major works' of
'high quality' (National Curriculum, English, 1995, p. 20), which allows pupils
in Wales to consider and 'read works by Welsh authors' and requires 'English
literary heritage' to be conveyed through the recommended texts. Bakhtin
(*ibid.*) refers to this as the 'absolute conclusiveness and closedness . . . of the
temporally valorized epic past' (p. 16). Even at 'A' level, where some scope
remains on some syllabi for invention, multiculturalism and difference to exist,
the tendency seems to be toward the centre ground, a monoglossic 'unitary
language' which is not,

> . . . but is always in essence posited . . . opposed to the realities of
> heteroglossia . . . a force for overcoming this heteroglossia, imposing
> specific limits to it, guaranteeing a certain maximum of mutual under-
> standing and crystalizing into a real, although still relative, unity — the
> unity of the reigning . . . 'correct language' . . . (*ibid.*, p. 270)

Surely such a centralized version of 'correct language', defined by certain
groups *for* others is counter to a productive, healthy and critical education
system that encourages relevant and broad thinking in its students and staff.
As Bakhtin knew, living under Stalin, what was preferable and vital was a
'multiplicity of social voices and a wide variety of their links and interrelationships (always more or less dialogized)' (*ibid.*, p. 263). Diversity, difference,
contest, dialogue are the watch-words of this approach, but crucially a willingness to acknowledge the 'links and interrelationships' across what Bakhtin
(*ibid.*) called 'the borderlines' (p. 29), brings us back to our concern for the
interdisciplinary method. How else can one indicate that cultural expression is
not a 'unitary, completely finished-off and indisputable language — it is . . . a
living mix of varied and opposing voices . . . developing and renewing itself'?
(Bakhtin, 1990, p. 49).

As Colin MacCabe explains, 'contemporary culture has been divided up
within those assumptions in ways that make it difficult if not impossible for
the universities to produce the kind of knowledge that is urgently required
if we are to understand better the world in which we live' (MacCabe, 1995,
p. 14). Similarly, Ernest Gombrich (1969) warns of the 'so-called disciplines
on which our academic organization is founded' which 'are no more than
techniques . . . means to an end, but no more than that' (p. 46). If the disciplines become straightjackets on the approaches one can take to texts, then
they have outlived their usefulness for a culture defined today by multifacetness
and diversity.

The failure to acknowledge the possibilities of interdisciplinarity were
spelled out by Tom Wolfe, who wrote

they've broken learning down into compartments — mathematics, history, geography, Latin, biology — it doesn't make sense to the tribal kids, it's like trying to study a flood by counting the trees going by; it's unnatural. (Wolfe in Stearn, 1968, p. 45)

Wolfe's 'tribal kids' are the technogenerations who have grown up knowing about and using new technologies until they become second nature to them. To them it is, therefore, 'unnatural' to experience education in discrete and artificial units and for technologies to be labelled as relevant only in certain of these areas — such as 'information technology' or 'word processing'. Education, at secondary and tertiary levels, must recognize these facts or risk the continuation of the problem identified by Paul Willis in 1990 wherein education 'will become almost totally irrelevant to the real energies and interests of most young people and have no part of their identity formation' (Willis quoted in Giroux and McLaren, 1994, p. 10). When Willis writes of the '"needs" of industry' becoming increasingly dominant in education, he relates it to a tension between education and 'technical instrumentalism' that he sees as a direct channel into a narrow, vocational interpretation of technology. I am suggesting ways of integrating such trends into a wider interdisciplinary teaching project that both involves the very 'energies' Willis feared were being drained away and the critical lessons of cultural/interdisciplinary studies.

The media technologies cross subject boundaries, bleed from one to another and can be a useful site for the discussion of the ways in which contemporary culture functions. That is, rather than just being a tool, technology can become central to the study itself, opening up a whole field of possible intertextual connections and contests that reflect the similar relations within the culture as a whole. How is technology used, by whom, in what forms? How is it represented to us and how can it be empowering or disempowering? Who has access, for how long and with what effects? The very similar group of questions that media studies has traditionally asked must now be extended to the broader media technologies: the computer, Internet, games, interactive television and so on. These activities, modes of expression and definers of identity are easily excluded from education, dismissed as either tools or leisure, as television once was, and yet the same positions hold true: 'all need elucidation, all need to be read as cultural texts, iconic in character, which can be decoded to reveal large numbers of meanings' (Masterman, 1980, p. 20). The development and widening of media studies to include the rise of technoculture provides further ways 'to understand what keeps making the lives we live, and the societies we live in . . .' (Hall quoted in Giroux and McLaren, 1994, p. 9).

The concept of interdisciplinarity is by no means a new one, but has tended to be much discussed then often brushed aside as the terrain of certain 'new' academic hybrids like American studies, media studies, women's studies and latterly cultural studies. It can, however, present opportunities to engage students in a range of studies that enable empowerment as well as intelligent and relevant critical perspectives, operating at 'the frontiers of intellectual life, pushing for new questions, new models and new ways of study' (*ibid.*, p. 2). As Henry Giroux and Peter McLaren have written, a cultural studies combining theory and practice is part of

> creating a new language, rupturing disciplinary boundaries, decentering authority, and rewriting the institutional and discursive borderlands in which politics becomes a condition for reasserting the relationship between agency, power and struggle. (Giroux and McLaren, 1994, p. ix)

What new technologies demonstrate is the everyday acceptance and generation of intertextuality, constantly repeating, mutating, intersecting and referring within itself to other phenomena. Thus the idea and culture of surfing has been adopted as both the language and iconic style for a section of the cyber-culture; its fluorescent board-colours have become the semiotic reference point for up-beat journals like *Wired* that are aimed at the Internet audience. The image-flow spills film into video games, cartoon comic book heroes into films, television into books in an endless media intertextuality, creating a new language which is complex, multi-layered and strangely alien to many. Education should get to know it because increasingly it is what our students know and will learn quickly and effectively. Teachers at all levels 'need to use our authority, mobilized through a pedagogy of risk and experimentation, to discover what the questions can be in the everyday lives of our students, and what political possibilities such questions open up' (Grossberg in Giroux and McLaren, 1994, p. 20). This will involve leaving the territory of the known, and being prepared to 'enter the terrain of everyday life . . . (to) prize open already existing contradictions' (*ibid.*, p. 20). The teacher must become 'the critical pedagogue . . . who teaches from where the student is, rather than from where the teacher is at . . . (and) respect the myriad expertise of the students that s/he does not share' (Mostern in Giroux and McLaren, 1994, p. 256). Within the strictly defined and barricaded borders of educational policy 'teachers become border-crossers through their ability to . . . make different narratives available to themselves and other students (and) . . . by legitimating difference as a basic condition for understanding the limits of one's own voice' (Giroux in Grossberg *et al.*, 1992, p. 206). Chantal Mouffe (1988) has written about citizenship in a way that can be applied to the idea of an ideal education as a 'community . . . a diverse collection of communities . . . a forum for creating unity without denying specificity' (p. 30).

Working with Technoculture

In the desire to be Giroux's border-crossers, teachers have to ensure their students are 'media literate in a world of changing representations' (in Grossberg *et al.*, 1992, p. 210), but also importantly acknowledge that students cross over into borders of meaning, maps of knowledge, social relations, and values that are increasingly being negotiated and rewritten as the codes and regulations which organize them become destabilized and reshaped. (Giroux in Natoli and Hutcheon, 1993, p. 482)

My feeling is that, in a substantial sense, students have discovered a terrain in which these processes take place — cyberculture or the realms of information and new media technologies. Here are the very borders of Giroux's theory, the meeting grounds of multiple identities, places, languages, images, points of view and so on, all competing for attention, awaiting our participation and interaction. It is 'a place where they felt recognized and included, where they could unite knowledge learned in classrooms with life outside' (hooks, 1994, p. 3). It is a place akin to William Gibson's imagined 'cyberspace':

A consensual hallucination experienced by billions of legitimate operators, in every nation, by children being taught mathematical concepts . . . A graphic representation of data . . . Unthinkable complexity . . . (Gibson, 1986, p. 67)

Approaches drawn from cultural studies, especially its border-crossing interdisciplinarity, could find a focus around the cluster of new technologies that Kellner (1995) terms 'media culture':

a form of technoculture that merges culture and technology in new forms and configurations, producing new types of societies in which media and technology become organizing principles. (p. 2)

— and be productive in its connection with the new places inhabited by students, best manifested as the Internet or the game-worlds of virtual reality.

At a recent event, *Media Waves*, in Brighton (England) which was examining changing attitudes and fears about just such a media culture, a most interesting comment came from the students themselves who, contrary to the dystopian doom and gloom from the academics, took a contrary position:

We are not dominated by technology. We know how to use it. We have developed ways of using it for our own needs. And the next generation will learn from us. (in Greenhalgh, 1995, p. iii)

They were 'taking the club experience and culture into areas of high culture' (*ibid.*), a reference to the techno revolution that has grown in and through the club and 'rave culture'. In this youth cultural sphere, technology has never been anything other than intrinsic to the experience which is, in certain respects, a 'multi-media' experience of light, sound, movement, heat and space.

As Sarah Thornton writes, 'various media are integral to youth's social and ideological formations' and not only form the rave experience itself, but are essential to the secretive organisation of the events, using 'micromedia' (flyers and listings), the music press and pirate radio to broadcast rave sites. As she argues, in this youth phenomenon 'media are there and effective right from the start' (Thornton in Ross and Rose, 1994, p. 176) and the 'underground' culture is in constant dialogue with the mainstream, relishing 'the attention conferred by media condemnation' (*ibid.*, p. 181), mutating its forms and sampling its technologies. The immense importance of the recording, transmission and reproduction of sounds and video to rave culture demonstrates the manner in which youth culture has always felt comfortable with media technology as long as it was able to use it, play with it and engage creatively with it. In the hands of others (teachers, parents, institutions) it can become oppressive, predictable and *boring*, but beyond them is a creative space of possibility. As Tricia Rose comments on black rappers too, it became a way of blurring distinctions 'between literate and oral modes of communication' through using technology to redefine 'the constitution of narrative originality, composition, and collective memory (and) . . . challenge institutional apparatuses that define property, technological innovation and authorship' (Rose, 1994, p. 85). Rap builds on the oral traditions of black culture, but uses technological innovations such as sampling and beat-boxes to create something new, a youth language that once again embraces technology. It is 'post-literate orality' in which ancient passing-on of stories is enhanced through technoculture's resources, so that sampling 'is a process of cultural literacy and intertextual reference' (*ibid.*, p. 89), crossing different musical genres for political, humorous or many other effects. The music is therefore dialogized through human and technological interfacing: 'It affirms black musical history and locates these "past" sounds in the "present"' (*ibid.*) but does it through engaging with technology:

> Rap technicians employ digital technology as instruments, revising black musical styles and priorities through the manipulation of technology. (*ibid.*, p. 96)

Rose calls this 'techno-black cultural syncretism', suggesting the 'simultaneous exchange' (*ibid.*), or what I term dialogue, that permeates youth's relationship to media technologies and that empowers them and gives them a voice.

In music, as in everyday life, the young are not necessarily technovictims, despite the image one often gains from adult discourse. The goggle-eyed, game-boy playing, video-watching, Walkman-wearing youth negotiates the terrains of technology with greater confidence and knowledge than most, if not all, adults, who are filled with technophobias.

> With a new technology like the computer, the major trick is to find its real wolf content underneath the sheep's wool of its ability to imitate old ways of doing things. (Kay, 1995, p. 24)

This 'wolf' has long been recognized and integrated into the everyday lives of the young, who are the citizens of this new territory of cyberspace or cyber-ville. This future-present place in which technology is central has been learned and mapped by the young, for whom the telephone is an accepted tool, while television, computer, radio and video are common-places of their world. The commercial market for virtual realities has entered the High Streets with 'Megazone' game centres, cyber-cafes and cyber-pubs in major cities all over England, but the effects are not necessarily negative:

> I believe that a kid raised with a joystick in his hand has a funda-mentally different appreciation for the image on the screen than you or I do. This is a kid who knows that the image on the screen is up for grabs. He has been empowered to change the picture on the screen . . . (Rushkoff, 1994)

> The thing I like about the Net is that it is boundary-less. It takes away many of the stereotypes people have about age or their sex . . . because it's purely on a communication level of ideas. (15-year-old 'cyber-brat' in Rushkoff, 1994)

Teaching must validate this variety of response to the contemporary cul-ture, not to incorporate it into the safety of the sanitized curriculum, but as a source of transdisciplinary possibility and intertextual investigation. We have to experience the multiple surfaces and depths of technology just as virtual reality (VR) lets you inside the machine itself, but remembering that in VR 'you can affect what happens . . . become part of that world . . . change it, and the changes occur as you make them' (Sherman and Judkins, 1992, p. 17).

Living in Cyber-ville

Cyber-ville seems a long way from Forster's Machine, but in one sense it is merely a shift of perception. To see technology as empowering and creative rather than destructive and negative is a major alteration, but one that stems in good measure from adopting youthful experience of the everyday. Cyber-punk writers grew out of youth sub-cultural groupings, especially rock cul-ture, and developed a view of technological society that refused the dystopian outlook in favour of a more sceptical, ambivalent position. Technology can be seen as good, fun, helpful, creative, productive as well as represented through all the terrible images inherited from science fiction visions of uncontrolled technolust and destruction. Discussions along these lines, integrating a variety of different texts, could be a productive method of opening certain questions about the human condition, our relations with technology, its construction (or not) of identities, its relationship to concepts of power, gender, race, globaliza-tion and so on. A specific way into the multifaceted issues I begin to sketch here might be through the work of cyberpunk writers — not as a retreat into a 'safe' medium, the novel, but as an accessible route forward into other connected areas of study.

Using William Gibson and Film

The 'inventor' of cyberspace, William Gibson, claims that the 'media' had more influence on him as a writer than fiction and his 'feelings about technology are *totally* ambivalent' (in McCaffery, 1993, pp. 265 and 274). He shares these feelings with much of his audience who have grown up with 'a joystick in their hands', surrounded by technology and using it in their everyday lives. For him too, life cannot be 'divided up into different *compartments*', with literature apart from 'television, music, film' (*ibid.*, p. 266), since all of them interact with one another in a transdisciplinary manner. Gibson's work is about the present viewed from the future in which media and technology have become central to the culture, suffusing the language itself. Gibson's *Neuromancer* opens with a startling image: 'The sky above the port was the color of television tuned to a dead channel' (1984, p. 9), and constantly uses other media-soaked metaphors, like 'hypnagogic images jerking past like film compiled from random frames . . . a blurred fragmented mandala of visual information' (*ibid.*, p. 68). His work is a 'complex synthesis of modern pop culture, high tech, and advanced literary technique' (Sterling in Gibson, 1993, p. 10) forming a web of information or 'matrix', rather like an elaborate version of a total Internet that Gibson's friend and co-author Bruce Sterling has written of as an

> 'expansive and seamless' Net of television-telephone-telex-tape recorder-VCR-laser disk . . . phone line, cable TV, fiber-optic cords hissing out words and pictures in torrents of pure light. All netted together in a web over the world, a global nervous system, an octupus of data.
> (Sterling, 1989, quoted in Penley and Ross, 1991, p. 299)

In Gibson's work, there is a 'polyglot mix of styles and cultures' (*ibid.*, p. 300) which has enormous appeal to students interested in a multiplicity of cultural expressions — MTV, pop culture, television, comics, novels, fashion, games and so on. His novels mix and match the fragments of contemporary culture into an almost recognizable new place, rather like the feeling one has sitting at a computer dipping in and out of the Internet, picking up information and graphics, alongside absurd notations and voices from everywhere. For Gibson and many cyber-writers, technology is an 'omnipresent, all-permeating, definitive force' which dramatizes 'the hidden bulk of an iceberg of social change' (Sterling in Gibson, 1993, p. 11), and yet their responses are not a traditional pure dystopianism in which a doom pervades the crucial meeting place of human and machine. In fact, as Sterling argues, one noticeable characteristic is 'its boredom with Apocalypse' (*ibid.*, p. 12). Most importantly, cyber-writing represents 'a decade that has finally found its own voice', argues Sterling (*ibid.*), and in so doing has gone some way to giving expression to the subterranean mutations and mixes of youth cultural expressions. Gibson and others like John Shirley, Pat Cadigan and Bruce Sterling, have fed off the sub-cultural styles and awarenesses to produce a vibrant and dynamic transgenre of writing that manages to cross-refer and intertextualize itself with a range of other forms and styles.

Cyber-punk writers see power as no longer in the hands of government, but with corporations, or what Gibson calls 'zaibatsus': 'multinationals that shaped the course of human history (and) had transcended old barriers . . . (and could) access vast banks of corporate memory' (Gibson, 1984, p. 242). Through his fiction he demonstrates that these users of technology can only be countered through a similar, if not better, understanding of the very same technology in the hands of the people. Again, it seems that the identification between youth and technology is a positive opportunity to empower and give a voice to those who so often feel cut adrift from decisions and processes of power and to break away from 'the paradigms print gave you' (Gibson, 1986, p. 204).[3] This may appear overly optimistic and somewhat fanciful, but it is an alternative reading of the machine/human relationship that does offer potential rather than apocalypse and democracy rather than dictatorship.

A student reading a Gibson novel is immediately making connections with cinema, to *Escape From New York*, and in particular *Blade Runner* (directed by Ridley Scott in 1982), and seeing the ways by which Gibson imagined a world, the Sprawl, in his novels.[4] Just as *Blade Runner* is a hybrid form, borrowing from different sources and describing a future-world of hierarchical structures of power, so is cyber-punk — part detective fiction, part rock-video, part sci-fi, but together creating some marvellous new genre. *Blade Runner* dramatizes the relationship of humanity and technology in an highly ambivalent manner, raising questions about the nature of humanity in the process. The film's 'cyborgs' or 'replicants' articulate arguments about identity, belonging and what has been done with technology in the contemporary world, whilst the film's extraordinary use of space and place suggests complex relations of power, ethnicity and gender. These are not easy texts to read, for they lead the reader along many routes the following of which demands critical reading skills which embrace more than any one discipline, but actively encourage a range of skills and a variety of connections to be made. To intercut from *Blade Runner* back to a Gibson story like *The Belonging Kind*, written with John Shirley, would be a very productive reading experience. The story too is concerned with issues of identity, home and belonging and centres on Coretti, ironically a lecturer in linguistics who cannot communicate with the world and longs to be a part of some community. The human realm offers him nothing but anxiety and he becomes fascinated by the cyborg, chameleon-girl whose identity is unfixed and ever-changing according to her surroundings. She literally embodies identity change and the capacity to find new subjectivities, 'shed like the skin of some fabulous animal' (Gibson, 1993, p. 62). Through her, Coretti is guided beyond the narrow dissatisfactions of his world, into something new, 'into a fragmented amalgam of conversations' (*ibid.*, p. 73) rather than the mundanity of a single voice. The story deliberately unsettles the reader, as it does Coretti, offering us none of the certainties and neat narrative closure of many stories, but instead, like *Blade Runner*, suggests something more complex and fragmented, more akin to the experience of life itself in the technoculture.

I would always encourage the interrelationship between visual narrative and writing as a very productive means of discussing different ways of addressing significant themes. For example, just as cyber-punk novels are concerned with ambivalent responses to media technologies and the tension between control and order, so are the popular *Terminator* films (1984 and 1991). The last words in the second film are:

> The unknown future rolls toward us. I face it for the first time with a sense of hope because if a machine, a Terminator, can learn the value of human life, maybe we can too.

The films are concerned with the relationship between humanity and machinery and suggest that a mutual 'learning' is possible. Their popularity is, in part I believe, to do with their rejection of simple readings of technology as dystopian in the same way that *Blade Runner* (1982) 'offers a mediation between technology and human values' (Ryan and Kellner in Kuhn, 1990, p. 62) when it presents an ambiguous relationship between Deckard and Rachel. Similarly, *Terminator 1* and *2* show technology being used in a wide variety of ways and for different purposes. The young hero, John Connor, has acquired technological skills and is seen using his microcomputer to steal (money from a cash machine) and to save (by breaking into a computer plant) — almost as if to demonstrate the possibility for good and evil contained within the technology itself and in those who use it. But the film's emphasis upon the young and the motifs of the future as something worth 'saving' indicates an underlying attention to possibility in the film.

The Terminator is set in the 1980s, and is saturated by machinery, screens, gadgets and automatons suggesting that 'the defence network computer (Skynet) of the future which decided our fate in a microsecond had its humble origins here, in the rather more innocuous technology of the film's present' (Penley in Kuhn, 1990, p. 117). This 'innocuous technology' is shown throughout the film as prone to break-down or to misuse, indicating that there may be nothing inherently bad about it, but rather in the ways it is used. For example, if we come to rely on it to make communication (the telephone, the beeper, the answering machine, etc.), what happens if the message gets blocked?

What the films propose is a learning process, signified by the merging of human and machine, so that Sarah becomes a 'hard body' and closer to the terminator's single-mindedness and rigour, whilst the Termintor in *T2* becomes 'humanized' — a parent to John Connor, who kills no one, but rather cares and saves. It is a 'partial and ambiguous merging of the two, a more complex response . . . (not) the Romantic triumph of the organic over the mechanical, or the nihilistic recognition that we have all become automata . . .' (*ibid.*, p. 118), but a recognition that culture can be reconceived, or reparented, in a way that acknowledges the central role of technology and yet maintains humanity too. This is a humanity transformed and no longer locked into a hopeless oppositional mentality, but one in which a variety of 'norms' have been questioned and alternatives proposed. This includes gender issues, since Sarah Connor is as confident with technology as anyone in the film and closely connected to the future itself, as well as with issues of power, authority and control, all of which are examined in the films. Technology, in the forms of automated factories, close both *Terminator* films and it is there that the Terminators 'die', in one crushed by a machine, in the other smelted down to its constituent parts, reminding the audience that it is all man-made and that technology is always an expression of our humanity, our responsibility, 'the machine is us, our processes, an aspect of our embodiment' (Haraway, 1991, p. 180). The horror of nuclear war, the Skynet program and the eery world of 'Cyberdyne Corporation', the Tyrrel Corporation (in *Blade Runner*) and Gibson's 'zaibatsus' are from the same scientific, technological minds that also produce the basic, ubiquitous technologies of everyday life. Just as we learn to control the everyday forms, we must educate ourselves and others to use and control those forms that seem always beyond us. Reading different technotexts in this way can contribute to this familiarity and to the vital interrogation of the ideological nature of the machine/human relationship, but in ways that step beyond the simplistic, mythic notion of apocalypse.

'Cyber-punk is really about the present' (Rucker, 1992, p. 9) and about the possible dangers of a 'monovocal capitalist ideology' (Fiske, 1987, p. 309), that speaks with one voice, but it also argues it can be reprogrammed through knowledge, participation and critique of the very technologies that appear to be dominant. In the hands of the young this may be possible because, as Rushkoff has said, 'a kid raised with a joystick in his hand has a fundamentally different appreciation for the image on the screen'; he feels comfortable with that image and the technology that created it and sees it as 'up for grabs'. In such a situation, one is 'empowered to change the picture on the screen' (Rushkoff, 1994):

> These kids aren't mind-boggled. These kids are natives in a land where the rest of us are immigrants, and these kids speak the language like natives and speak it better than you or I can ever hope to. This is their culture and I think it's we who have to look to them to how to navigate . . . through this terrain not they who should be looking to us.

This 'language' is, of course, complex, interdisciplinary, and hybrid, a heteroglossic mix of reading skills, image-analysis, technospeak and many other highly integrated but dynamic forces. In cyber-punk fiction and cyber-culture this language enables and empowers the 'streets to speak' (Lucius Shepard in Wolmark, 1994, p. 111). To acquire these skills and to develop them will be increasingly essential in education, for this is already becoming the language of contemporary cultures.

A 'New Subjectivity'?

The French critic, Jean Baudrillard wrote 'It is not necessary to write science fiction' because we are in it (quoted in Bukatman, 1993, p. 182), and it is through cyber-writers that this has become most apparent. Indeed, cyber-punk's innovative form 'is to traditional narrative as MTV is to the feature film' (Slusser in McCaffrey, 1993, p. 334), with its 'optical prose' (*ibid.*) full of sharp, condensed, cut-up surfaces and intertextual mixes of different popular cultural forms. Rejecting, as William Gibson does, the label of science fiction, he writes instead about 'the world in which we live' (quoted in Kellner, 1995, p. 299) embracing media technology, as both threatening and full of opportunities for a redefinition of the human. In the 1960s, Marshall McLuhan wrote of 'electric technology' as a means to extend 'our central nervous system itself in a global embrace . . . (in a) technological simulation of consciousness' (McLuhan, 1965, p. 3), and by Gibson's time, the electric, media technology impacts upon the human in equally ambiguous ways, suggesting a 'double articulation in which we both find the end of the subject and a new subjectivity constructed at the computer station or television screen' — a 'terminal identity' (Bukatman, 1993, p. 9).

Through Gibson we have arrived in the borderlands I wrote of earlier, where disciplines collide, where the traditional notions of 'object' and 'subject' blur, and new positions have to be found in order to navigate its terrain. In this new space of possibility, educational dialogue can become 'liminal transformation' (Haraway, 1991, p. 177), where the concept of liminality, borrowed from the work of Victor Turner (1974), suggests being 'liberated from normative demands . . . betwixt and between successive lodgements . . . In this gap between ordered worlds (where) almost anything can happen' (pp. 13–14). The technosphere represented by cyber-punk, the Internet, and the interface of human and machine can be liberating in this way, as if lying outside the grip of the 'norm', curiously 'unterritorialized' and so existing beyond the known, fixed territories of the education mainstream, 'unincorporated into the system of controlled, civilized spaces' (Shields, 1991, p. 84).

This is very close to Donna Haraway's notion of the 'cyborg', the space in which human and machine interact and merge. I would suggest that the young are closer to this 'New Edge' or 'limen' (threshold) and, therefore, more immediately capable of benefitting from this new subjectivity which might offer a 'subversive reconception of the subject that situates the human and the technological as coextensive, codependent, and mutually defining' (*ibid.*, p. 22), rather than as simply oppressive, conditioning and reductive.

In the creative hands of the young, new technologies are in dialogue with the human and not just defined as a threat, or a controlling force, as with Forster's Machine, but in flux and process, predicated on invention and mutability. Surely, however difficult this terrain appears to be from the outside, from the inside, where the young are, it is exciting and full of possibility and very similar to Haraway's definition of science fiction as 'concerned with the interpenetration of boundaries between problematic selves and unexpected others and . . . the exploration of possible worlds' (in Grossberg *et al.*, 1992, p. 300). In the science fiction 'reality' of technoculture, the young are mapping the terrain, speaking the language and should be encouraged to explore these 'possible worlds' in relation to their mainstream education.

Donna Haraway's 'cyborg' names this 'new subjectivity' emerging from the human-technological mix in which the two are wedded together and interfused. Technology in this argument is not demonized but embraced as the means to 'reconstructing the boundaries of daily life, in partial connection to others, in communication with all of our parts' (in Penley and Ross, 1991, p. 308). Thus, 'cyborg imagery can suggest a way out of the maze of dualisms in which we have explained our bodies and our tools to ourselves' (*ibid.*). Education must try to understand the full potential of technology and pay close attention to all its facets so that we can 'look for ways to subvert and turn (it) to new liberatory uses' (Fitting, *ibid.*).[5]

Towards a Cyborg Education?

The 'fruitful coupling' (Haraway, 1991, p. 150) of human and technological can be part of what Douglas Kellner (1979) refers to as 'emancipatory cultural production' (p. 42) because it transgresses the boundaries that fix people into set ways of thinking and acting. Just as the Internet might emancipate, democratize and globalize, so might other technologies empower us to reassess how we respond to the world and raise questions about how we are positioned within it. Donna Haraway (1991) argues for a 'cyborg world' where, rather than clinging on to a traditional view rooted in the idea of technical domination and the call back to an 'imagined organic body to integrate our resistance' (p. 154), we must make 'a perverse shift of perspective' which engages us more fully within 'technologically mediated societies' (*ibid.*). As she says, 'single vision produces worse illusions than double vision or many-headed monsters' (*ibid.*) and so we must try to push beyond the limited and fearful perceptions of technology and adopt instead the fluidity and complexity of the cyborg. Haraway is particularly concerned with the need to challenge notions of gender, but her theory helps to frame new attitudes to technology in general. As she writes, the contemporary, post-modern world cannot maintain an 'anti-science metaphysics, a demonology of technology', but must find ways of 'embracing the skilful task of reconstructing the boundaries of daily life . . . Cyborg imagery can suggest a way out of the maze of dualisms in which we have explained our bodies and our tools to ourselves' (*ibid.*, p. 181). Whatever engages the mind into a discussion of these issues will raise the profile of the arguments themselves, for 'to "press enter" is not a fatal error, but an inescapable possibility for changing maps of the world' (Haraway in Grossberg, *et al.*, 1992, p. 327).

Above all, what Haraway sees in the potential of human-machine connection is 'a powerful infidel heteroglossia' (Haraway, 1991, p. 181), that is, a means of many voices speaking out or finding a space for their articulation in the new technologies of the late twentieth century. Media technology has for so long been defined as centripetal, that is, forcing everything towards the centre, towards a one-voiced, monolithic control. What Haraway proposes is centrifugal, diverse and multi-voiced. The use, study, pleasure, critique of and active engagement with technology I have proposed in this chapter can be related to Haraway's project and to the emancipatory possibilities of technology. Indeed it is vital to the struggle for empowerment and expression that we work with and through technology to teach and learn what the Terminator learns, 'the value of human life'.

Conclusion — 'We're all Cyborgs Now'[6]

Besides, revolution would not begin, do you think, with an act of murder — wars might begin in that way — but with teaching. (Walker, 1976, p. 192)

We live in 'a culture tattooed by digital reality' (Kroker, 1992, p. 165) and our teaching must engage with it at various points, using its attractions, effects and problems as avenues for exploration and discussion. Cyber-punk can be seen as a 'natural extension of elements already present in science fiction' (Sterling, 1986, p. xii), exploring 'the interface between human and machine in order to focus on the general question of what it means to be human' (Wolmark, 1994, p. 110). This issue is central to the education process and can be addressed in many different ways, and a reconsideration of literacy must be a significant part of the process. What I attempt to suggest here is that critical engagement with technology in various ways, through its representations largely, but also through its practices (employing interdisciplinary openness) can be a productive and stimulating experience for students and simultaneously raise a range of vitally important social and cultural questions.

Rick Rylance (1994) has pointed out that computer technology has already altered the way we respond to texts, placing them side by side, interweaving them and tracing connections and patterns (p. 90), so that 'the boundaries between text and commentary are now porous' (*ibid.*). Students skilled in the technosphere have less reverence for print-literacy perhaps, but can read a wider range of texts in new and different ways, reading across, between and through them in order to gain insights that print alone may not provide. In this 'healthy riot' (*ibid.*, p. 91) of possibility, reading alters, becoming multidimensional and transdisciplinary, generating 'empowered delight' (*ibid.*, p. 92) in the field of textual interplay which forms part of the wider cultural environment. For if we view culture as a contested terrain (see Jordan and Weedon, 1995), then its texts will be similarly contesting for our attention and for authority through their meanings. Educators can facilitate the engagement with these contested meanings using the materials that students are already concerned about in their everyday lives as a medium for cultural studies. It is not imagined as a closed world of study, but a gateway to a broader set of issues that emerge around the subject of technology and the human, issues of gender, race, power and hegemony. The aim is for a route into 'multiperspectival cultural studies' which avoids 'one-sidedness, orthodoxy, and cultural separatism by stressing the need to adopt a wide range of perspectives to understand and interpret cultural phenomena' (Kellner, 1995, p. 97).

Technology, viewed within a critical, interrogative framework, can be liberatory, signifying 'the end of the subject and a new subjectivity' (Bukatman, 1993, p. 9). Students can be empowered to analyze and resist the 'subject' given and constructed within the social order, of which education is a part, and cross over through technological engagement into a new subjectivity that acknowledges their skills, offers new modes of expression and encourages the exploration of new terrains of intertextual reading. Without sounding overly utopian, for that is an old trap to fall into, education cannot retreat into Forster's Machine or compartmentalize technology into discrete subject-units, for it permeates everything we do and, more importantly, everything our students do and know. Technology cannot be ignored, for to do this would be to hand over our selves to the machine, as in Forster's story, until 'the entire communication-system broke down, all over the world, and the world, as they understood it, ended' (Forster in Barnes and Egford, 1973, p. 163). To resist this 'silence' (*ibid.*, p. 164) — of the technological machine stopped — we must accept and learn to live with it, not passively, but actively, since,

> The same technology that will hardwire a pilot into the computer that flies the jet and enables the missiles will allow our friend, hit by a speeding truck, to walk again. There is no choice between utopia and dystopia, Good Terminator or Evil Terminator — they are both here. (Hables, Gray and Mentor in Brahm and Driscoll, 1995, p. 243)

To borrow from John Law (1991), education 'might work towards a form of modest, multivocal organization, where all could be reborn as hopeful monsters — as places where the necessary incompatibilities, inconsistencies and overlaps come gently and creatively together' (p. 19). In this realm of learning, a new space has been created, recognizing a post-modern, decentred, 'multivocal' culture in which 'they are both here' can become a genuine possibility around which to structure approaches to education.

We are learning to inhabit this permeable body, whether the one we walk around in or the one we are told to vote in, and to experience a range of virtual realities, some of which we can imagine enjoying, passing on to our cyborg children. Perhaps after all, we just need to learn cyborg family values — good maintenance, technical expertise, pleasure dispersed and multiple, community R&D, improved communication. (Brahm and Driscoll (1995), p. 243)

Our 'cyborg children' already occupy this new space and it is important to enter it with them, learn about it, criticize it, but above all have a dialogue with it through education. Dialogism aims at 'the rupturing and dislocation of the seamless whole of the monologic world of objects, events and consciousnesses through the introduction of heterogeneous and multiform "materials" into the text' (Gardiner, 1992, p. 25), and it is only through the continual revision and reconstruction of 'literacy' and teaching approaches that this can be achieved in education. Ultimately, it is not, as Forster suggested, the Machine that will end the world, but our unwillingness to engage with it and our failure to enter this dialogue, for as Bakhtin (1984) wrote, 'To be means to communicate dialogically. When dialogue ends, everything ends. Thus dialogue . . . cannot and must not come to an end' (p. 252).

Notes

1 I recognize that this chapter makes certain assumptions about access to technology in education and everyday life that may not be true for all students. However, the point is that even if the sophistication of the Internet is still relatively unavailable to all, other forms of interconnected technologies are: Nintendo, Sega, microcomputers, Megazone Game Centres, etc. The knowledges I am writing about begin there.

2 There is inadequate space in this chapter to discuss all the teaching strategies that could be adopted, at different levels, but my intention is to theorize the possibilities and to offer some guidance here.

3 A recent report of children's reading *One Week in March: A Survey of the Literature Children Read* by the School Curriculum and Assessment Authority suggested that 'children read less and less widely as their education progresses', from a range of 132 authors in year 3 to only twenty-seven by year 11 (16-year-olds), and by year 8 few studied texts from other cultures than British. SCAA chief executive, Nick Tate, said that 'a balance of reading is essential', but was concerned that too much attention to the contemporary was a shift too far in one direction (*The Times Educational Supplement*, 15 December 1995, p. 1).

4 Hollywood has begun a dramatic onslaught into certain aspects of technoculture and this will further the possibilities for interdisciplinary examinations of the representations of technology in a range of texts. Currently there are twenty cyberspace/ Internet films in production in Hollywood with *The Net* (directed by Irwin Winkler, 1995) being the first. Coming are the film of William Gibson's *Johnny Mnemonic* (directed by Robert Longo, 1995), *Strange Days* (directed by Kathryn Bigelow, 1996) and *Hackers* (directed by Iain Softley, 1996). However, these films persist in

'technofear' and suggest that 'Tinseltown is just using this new development as plot device to hang an action thriller on' (Phillips, 1995, p. 14). Films, despite *Blade Runner*, continue to see only the dark side of technology.

5   The feminist implications of technology are important and Donna Haraway's theory engages with this directly, as do the female cyber-writers, Pat Cadigan, Octavia Butler and others (see Wolmark, 1994). But the dialogue with technology may also liberate gender identity in interesting new ways akin to those desired in French feminist critic Helene Cixous's work:

> Where the wonder of being several and turmoil is expressed . . . she surprises herself at seeing, being, pleasuring in her gift of changeability. I am spacious singing Flesh: onto which is grafted no one knows which I — which masculine or feminine, more or less human but above all living, because *changing* I. (Cixous, 1994, p. 45)

> She slipped out of the self, she had that severity, that violent patience, she went by decollage, by radiance, by laying bare the senses, it requires unclothing sight all the way down to naked sight, it requires *removing from sight the looks that surround*, shedding the looks that demand, like tears, disregarding to arrive at sight without a project, contemplation . . . Sense flow, circulate, *messages as divinely complicated as the strange microphonetic signals*, conveyed to the ears from the blood, tumults, calls, inaudible answers vibrate, *mysterious connections are established* . . . at moments, harmonies of incalculable resonance occur. (*ibid.*, pp. 91–2)

6   Brahm and Driscoll (1995), p. 1.

References

BAKHTIN, M. (1984) *Rabelais and His World*, Bloomington, IN, Indiana University Press.

BAKHTIN, M.M. (1990) *The Dialogic Imagination*, Austin, TX, University of Texas Press.

BARNES, D. and EGFORD, R.F. (1973) *Twentieth-century Short Stories*, London, Harrap.

BARTHES, R. (1976) *Mythologies*, London, Paladin.

BRAHM, G. and DRISCOLL, M. (Eds) (1995) *Prosthetic Territories: Politics and Hypertechnologies*, Boulder, Westview Press.

BUKATMAN, S. (1993) *Terminal Identity: The Virtual Subject in Post-modern Science Fiction*, London, Duke University Press.

CIXOUS, H. (1994) *The Helene Cixous Reader*, London, Routledge.

DONALD, J. (1980) *Media Studies: Possibilities and Limitations*, London, BFI Education.

FISKE, J. (1987) *Power Plays Power Works*, London, Routledge.

FOUCAULT, M. (1972) *The Archaeology of Knowledge and the Discourse on Language*, New York, Pantheon.

FOUCAULT, M. (1977) *Discipline and Punish: The Birth of the Prison*, Harmondsworth, Penguin.

GARDINER, M. (1992) *The Dialogics of Critique: M.M. Bakhtin and the Theory of Ideology*, London, Routledge.

GIBSON, W. (1986) *Neuromancer*, London, Grafton Books.

GIBSON, W. (1993) *Burning Chrome*, London, Grafton Books.

GIROUX, H. (1992) 'Resisting difference: Cultural studies and the discourse of critical pedagogy' in GROSSBERG, L. *et al.* (Eds) *Cultural Studies*, London, Routledge.

GIROUX, H. (1993) 'Post-modernism as border pedagogy: Redefining the boundaries of race and ethnicity' in NATOLI, J. and HUTCHEON, L. (Eds) *A Post-modern Reader*, New York, Columbia University Press.

GIROUX, H. and McLAREN, P. (Eds) (1994) *Between Borders: Pedagogy and the Politics of Cultural Studies*, London, Routledge.

GOMBRICH, E.H. (1969) *In Search of Cultural History*, Oxford, Oxford University Press.

GREENHALGH, T. (1995) 'Surf's up on the media beach', *The Times Higher Educational Supplement*, 10 November, p. iii.

GROSSBERG, L. *et al.* (1992) *Cultural Studies*, London, Routledge.

GROSSBERG, L. (1994) 'Introduction: Bringin' it all back home — Pedagogy and cultural studies' in GIROUX, H. and McLAREN, P. (Eds) *Between Borders: Pedagogy and the Politics of Cultural Studies*, London, Routledge.

HARAWAY, D. (1991) *Simians, Cyborgs and Women: The Reinvention of Nature*, London, Free Association Books.

HARAWAY, D. (1992) 'The promises of monsters: A regenerative politics for inappropriate/d others' in GROSSBERG, L. (Ed.) *Cultural Studies*, London, Routledge.

hooks, b. (1994) *Outlaw Culture: Resisting Representations*, London, Routledge.

JORDAN, G. and WEEDON, C. (1995) *Cultural Politics*, London, Harvester Wheatsheaf.

KAY, A. (1995) 'Unleash the wolf from woolly thinking', *The Times Educational Supplement*, 23 June, p. 24.

KELLNER, D. (1979) 'T.V., ideology and emancipatory popular culture', *Socialist Review*, **45**, (May–June), pp. 37–65.

KELLNER, D. (1995) *Media Culture: Cultural Studies, Identity Politics Between the Modern and the Postmodern*, London, Routledge.

KROKER, A. (1992) *The Possessed Individual: Technology and Postmodernity*, London, MacMillan.

KUHN, A. (Ed.) (1990) *Alien Zone: Cultural Theory and Contemporary Science Fiction Cinema*, London, Verso.

LAW, J. (Ed.) (1991) *The Sociology of Monsters: Essays on Power, Technology and Domination*, London, Routledge.

LEIGH STAR, S. (Ed.) (1995) *The Cultures of Computing*, Oxford, Blackwell.

MacCABE, C. (1995) 'Masters of many universes', *The Times Higher Educational Supplement*, 24 March, p. 14.

McCAFFERY, L. (Ed.) (1993) *Storming the Reality Studio: A Casebook of Cyberpunk and Post-modern Fiction*, London, Duke University Press.

McLUHAN, M. (1965) *Understanding Media*, New York, McGraw Hill.

MASTERMAN, L. (1980) *Teaching About Television*, London, MacMillan.

MOSTERN, K. (1994) 'Decolonization as learning: Practice and pedagogy in Frantz Fanon's revolutionary narrative' in GIROUX, H. and McLAREN, P. (Eds) *Between Borders: Pedagogy and the Politics of Cultural Studies*, London, Routledge.

MOUFFE, C. (1988) 'The civics lesson', *The New Statesman*, 7 October, p. 28.

PEIM, N. (1993) *Critical Theory and the English Teacher*, London, Routledge.

PENLEY, C. (1990) 'Time travel, primal scene and critical dystopia' in KUHN, A. (Ed.) *Alien Zone: Cultural Theory and Contemporary Science Fiction Cinema*, London, Verso.

PENLEY, C. and Ross, A. (Eds) (1991) *Technoculture*, Minneapolis, University of Minnesota.

Neil Campbell

PHILLIPS, A. (1995) 'The ultimate paradox', *The Web*, November/December, pp. 14–17.
RABINOW, P. (Ed.) (1986) *The Foucault Reader*, Harmondsworth, Penguin.
ROSE, T. (1994) *Black Noise: Rap Music and Black Culture in Contemporary America*, Hanover, Wesleyan University Press.
RUCKER, R. (Ed.) (1992) *A User's Guide to Mondo 2000*, London, Thames 7 Hudson.
RUSHKOFF, D. (1994) 'Once upon a time in cyberville', *Equinox*, Channel 4 Television.
RYLANCE, R. (1994) *Roland Barthes*, London, Harvester Wheatsheaf.
SHERMAN, B. and JUDKINS, P. (1992) *Glimpses of Heaven, Visions of Hell: Virtual Reality and its Implications*, London, Hodder & Stoughton.
SHIELDS, R. (1991) *Places on the Margin: Alternative Geographies of Modernity*, London, Routledge.
SLUSSER, G. (1993) 'Literary MTV' in McCAFFERY, L. (Ed.) *Storming the Reality Studio: A Casebook of Cyberpunk and Post-modern Fiction*, London, Duke University Press.
STEARN, G. (Ed.) (1968) *McLuhan Hot and Cool*, Harmondsworth, Penguin.
STERLING, B. (Ed.) (1986) *Mirrorshades*, London, Harper Collins.
THORNTON, S. (1994) in Ross, A. and Rose, T. (Eds) (1994) *Microphone Fiends: Youth Music and Youth Culture*, London, Routledge.
TURNER, V. (1974) *Dramas, Fields and Metaphors*, New York, Cornell University Press.
WALKER, A. (1976) *Meridian*, London, Woman's Press.
WOLMARK, J. (1994) *Aliens and Others: Science Fiction, Feminism and Post-modernism*, London, Harvester Wheatsheaf.

Films

Blade Runner (1982) directed by Ridley Scott
Terminator (1984) directed by James Cameron
Terminator 2: Judgement Day (1991) directed by James Cameron

Section 3

Books, Literacy and Other Things

7 Reading More than Print

Ed Marum

Behind the Child and Her Book

This book has, up to this point, been concerned to bring together some individual perspectives on contemporary issues in literacy studies, seen from policy, teaching and research perspectives. In this short chapter I should like to begin to draw together what my own sense of these issues is and to highlight what seem to me to be some important questions for the future of literacy studies arising from them.

Thus far, we have tended in this volume to speak about children and books in an abstract and general sense; this is predictable, given the scope and range of the issues which have been under discussion. However, I should now like to attempt to link the issues arising from the first two sections more particularly to reading and to the practical activities of children.

The contributors have shown that there a number of issues to do with the experience of reading which one might highlight as important in the contemporary 'literacy arena' and which continue to merit further elaboration and research. Among these are the relationships between the politics of policy-making and planning at national levels and the 'delivery' of literacy programmes, however historically and culturally defined, at school and institutional levels — a point emerging clearly from Section 1. The character and nature of recent historical social developments and technological change have necessitated a clear need for Western governments to rethink their literacy programmes in broader social and cultural global perspectives than has been the case thus far.

Section 2 has pointed up the need for institutions to offer a clear and coherent rationale for the teaching of 'literature' within the institutional framework which embraces social as well as educational perspectives in the definition and teaching of literacies. 'Education is a social event', say Rijlaarsdam and Janssen. The process of self-evaluation which is inextricably bound up with the reading act offers readers the opportunity for thoughtful reflection upon the nature of the reading experience which quantitative, norm-referenced systems of evaluation, by their very nature, are incapable of recognizing or considering. If 'subject-reflexive action' (Witkin, 1981) is the foundation of an intelligence of feeling, it must in future have an increased role in the learning experience which reading is. Beyond this, our very understanding of 'reading' in its social and cultural context needs reappraisal, as Campbell makes clear in his exploration of the educational possibilities inherent in the study of non-print texts, their relationship with media technologies and the implications for future interdisciplinary study of 'the text'. In the foreground, standing against the backcloth of these gathered issues, is the young child and her book.

Teaching Beyond Print

We have recognized for some time that literacy begins and is well advanced before children undertake any formal schooling. Nursery rhymes, fairy stories, bedtime tales, and so on, make reading an early and enjoyable experience and teach us about ourselves and the world we are in. These early childhood activities have taught us for centuries and will, I am sure, continue to do so; in doing so they embark us upon our lifelong reading journey (Jenny Marum, 1995) and teach us who we are. Reading, like education, is a social event.

When we watch television or a film, stand at the bus stop, wait at the railway station, sit down with our comics, walk a trolley round the supermarket, we are of course learning to read and we continue to do so through life. The contexts of reading are multiple, and contexts help define different types of literacies. The world into which the young are growing is one of increasing technological change, and for this reason alone (and there are others of course) literacy, says Meek (1991) 'isn't what it used to be'. The majority of children learn to read before they can decipher the words in a book. This means that, in turn, the place of the book in literacy development is also a changing one, a fact that teachers of early years children are more than aware of when they plan and deliver their literacy programmes.

And yet as children advance through schooling, through their junior and secondary education, questions remain as to the type and quality of the experiences they encounter. How many schools can claim, for example, to have developed coherent literacy programmes which touch both the hearts and the minds of their children, which are demonstrably developmental, involve regular self-assessment and embrace the interdisciplinary study of literacies in a variety of contexts? As an ex-schoolteacher who has taught in both rural and urban schools, I was not successful in achieving such a programme. I believe my experience is not uncommon. Yet twenty years ago it became fashionable to talk about implementing policies for language across the curriculum; such notions persist today, in various forms and sometimes in different nomenclature. The reality of schooling is of course different, for the many reasons that we all know. Within the state school system, most teachers are also caught, obliged to deliver national policies and syllabuses which lack clearly-defined philosophical, practical and assessment procedures and which, in the respects we have outlined in this book, do not sufficiently touch their own or children's lives. Since the approaches taken to literacy are indistinguishable from the general approaches taken to learning, it is time for some radical reappraisal. This is not a counsel of perfection; it is a plea for the necessary rethinking of both educational policy and practice.

It remains the fact that it is largely within the context of formal schooling that the reading journeys we will take in our lives are shaped. Over twenty years ago Purves (1973) undertook a major study of 'literature education' in ten countries, examining children's 'patterns of response' to literature. Among his findings, he makes the following statements:

> ... these patterns are equally a function of the age of the students regardless of the country in which they reside ... (they) would tend to argue for a developmental or an educational view of the differences between ages ... Response to literature is a learned behaviour, this study seems to find. It is modified by what the student reads and it is affected by his culture, and presumably, by his school as an inculcator of that culture. Response to literature might be said to be a 'cognitive style', a way of thinking about literary experience, a way of ordering that thinking for discourse. If it is learned, the curriculum maker must then deal with the question of what is to be learned. (pp. 314–5)

Later reading-response theorists and commentators have gone on to develop lines of enquiry relating to the classroom experience of children. Marshall (1986), for example, undertook a small-scale study of children's classroom talk about their literary responses, and found that

> ... in both their oral and written work, these students were seldom encouraged to make or elaborate upon their personal reactions to literature. To a large extent, the process of learning about literature was a process of learning what to say about literature — and then saying it in the appropriate form ... students do have personal reactions and, although their expression is only rarely supported in class, such reactions play an important role in shaping what students may finally learn about literature and literary response. (p. 53)

We have seen that Janssen and Rijlaarsdam (chapter 5 in this volume) have added a contemporary perspective upon this important issue, and have gone on to suggest ways in which practice might be improved.

But we also know now that the early experience of schooling can be hugely formative of attitudes as, for example, national surveys undertaken in Britain by the Assessment and Performance Unit (APU) have shown. The APU conducted surveys between 1979 and 1983, using sub-samples of 1200 children to answer questions relating to their perceptions of reading and writing. Among their findings are the following:

> The findings suggest that the patterns of response established at age 11 not only influence outcomes at age 15, but are likely to be in evidence from the earliest school years ... Nine out of ten 11-year-olds

claimed to enjoy reading. Their answers indicated that they particularly enjoyed reading stories . . . The secondary surveys provide evidence of a somewhat diminished enthusiasm for reading among pupils of both sexes, as compared with 11-year-old pupils . . . The one common feature between the books listed as being most popular among this sub-sample (15-year-old boys) was the fact that they were stories that are more likely to be found in high street shops than in class libraries . . . Given a choice between fiction and non-fiction, a significantly lower proportion of secondary pupils than primary pupils preferred to read fiction . . . (APU, 1987, pp. 3–15)

Again, and significantly, we have the recent smaller-scale, snapshot survey undertaken by the SCAA (1995) as to what children read in school. I briefly discussed some of the issues arising from this in chapter 2 of this volume. In the context of schooling, and of the issues raised about our definitions of and approaches towards literacy, the analysis made by Moffett (1968) nearly thirty years ago continues to have a particular contemporary resonance:

The very subject matter of fiction inevitably concerns the making and breaking of communication among people, someone's learning or failure to learn, or something about discrepancies and adjustments of perspective . . . Stories both are systems of communications and knowledge, and are about such systems. Good art, as we all know, weds form to content, either through the dissonance of irony or the consonance of harmony. What makes such fusions possible is that our ways of apprehending and sharing experience are themselves a crucial part of what we call experience. (p. 149)

Over the last three decades our educational theory and practice has embraced a learning continuum from stories to narratives to genres to literacies. While we acknowledge that recent history has taught us the need to redefine literature and literacy in a new, contemporary social framework, and hence in the context of interdisciplinary multiliteracies, the question Purves raised in 1973 remains today; that is, 'what is to be learned?' It is the question which has now to be directed towards national policy-makers, educational practitioners and researchers, as well as to the children and youth of our world.

References

APU (1987) *Pupils' Attitudes to Reading*, London, NFER-Nelson.
MARSHALL, J.D. (1986) 'Classroom discourse and literary response' in NELMS, B. (Ed.) *Literature in the Classroom: Readers, Texts and Contexts*, Urbana, IL, NCTE.
MARUM, J. (1995) 'Encouraging wider reading: Classroom strategies' in MARUM, E. (Ed.)

Towards 2000: The Future of Childhood, Literacy and Schooling, London, Falmer Press.

MEEK, M. (1991) *On Being Literate*, London, Bodley Head.

MOFFETT, J. (1968) *Teaching the Universe of Discourse*, Boston, MA, Houghton-Mifflin.

PURVES, A.C. (1973) *Literature Education in Ten Countries*, New York, John Wiley.

SCAA (1995) *One Week in March: A Survey of the Literature Pupils Read*, London, SCAA, December.

WITKIN, R. (1981) *The Intelligence of Feeling*, London, Heinemann Educational.

8 A Tentative Non-conclusion

Ed Marum

The title of this piece is an acknowledgment of the uncertainties surrounding the debate on what we mean by literacy, which will certainly continue in future years; it is also a reaffirmation of Williams's view that culture, in any contemporary meaning, 'marks the effort at total qualitative assessment, but what it indicates is a process not a conclusion' (Williams, 1958). I take literacy to be an aspect of culture, and a fundamentally important one, using 'culture' again in the sense that Sarland (1991) has expressed it: 'the making of meaning and value, the sharing of knowledge, opinion and prejudice, and the delineation of a shared emotional response to the world and its artefacts'. The process of meaning-making is part of what it is to be human; literacy is fundamental human meaning-making.

Because it is a fundamental human activity, I said in the introduction to this book that literacy is not the sole province of teachers — the phrasing was deliberate and double-edged. In one sense, I am saying what is obvious — that others than teachers are involved in the study and teaching of literacy: parents, nursery leaders, playgroup organizers, childminders, psychologists, researchers, etc., and that these are among those who have important parts to play in further developing our understanding of what literacies mean in different communities and how schools can improve their literacy practice.

All the contributors to this book have made the point in different ways that we need to have strategies for acknowledging and teaching multiple perspectives on literacy in society: in this sense, too, literacy cannot be teachers' territory alone. Literacy begins before schooling begins, and continues throughout our lives, beyond schooling.

In another sense, however, I am also saying that teachers (and I am speaking of English teachers in particular in this context) are concerned not only with literacy, but are also necessarily concerned with a host of other issues, inevitably taking on other roles in their work in addition to that of teaching 'literacy'. This is inescapable, given that they are institutional members of the school community, with managerial, administrative, pastoral and other responsibilities. They are often teaching programmes of study devised and written by others, and they interpret such programmes in the light of national, regional and local concerns and interests. For many teachers, the additional business of testing and examinations is also a daily factor in their considerations; for those following examination syllabuses, the syllabus itself will often dictate what, and sometimes when, they will teach. The syllabus or study programme will also have an impact upon how they will teach, as will the mundane but equally important features of the school — buildings, rooms, other available accommodation and facilities, resource levels, and so on. I mention all of these here because they have an important influence upon the teacher's sense of her role and function, as well as upon her ability and competence to fulfil it in the situation in which she daily finds herself. The routine exigencies of school life, together with the multifaceted demands made upon teachers, of course in practice partly condition their sense of themselves, both personally and professionally. What does all this have to do with literacy?

In order to answer this question, I shall refer again to my introduction, when I said that the teacher will continue to be an important influence upon our definition of literacy and a central agent in its mediation in learning. The writers of this book have primarily been concerned to describe their perspectives on literacy issues in the state school sector, for that is where the vast bulk of our children are currently educated and taught, and where they will continue to be taught in the future, and it is from whence the majority of higher education students will continue to emerge. I want to suggest, therefore, that the future of literacy is inextricably bound up with the future of the state school system. In terms of policy and planning, as we have attempted to indicate, this has implications for national governments which they will need to address very speedily. For if education is to be concerned with maximizing quality of experience for children, it needs to be provided in circumstances which enable the best possible experience — this must also include teachers. If literacy as a fundamental area of the school curriculum is to become ever more important, as I believe is clearly the case, given the increasing social demands for more complex literacy abilities, then (to repeat once again from my introduction) it is important that the teacher has both a view of what literacy means and a strategy for its teaching. If today's society expects multiliterate abilities in all young people, tomorrow's society will assume them: the social, political and economic implications of non-possession will be very considerable.

The issues surrounding literacy are large and socially pervasive. We have seen that in contemporary society it is a multidisciplinary entity, and that it impinges upon our sense of history, psychology, politics, culture and education: it is to do with interpreting our own and others' languages and perspectives, with all the difficulties attaching to that process. It is also to do with individuals' beliefs, attitudes and values, with their sense of themselves and the meanings they make in the world. All of us have a literacy history which is part of us and which we carry forwards into the future, even as that future changes around us; it is a personal experience wholly unique and valuable. The sharing of that experience helps us learn as well as helps us teach:

These young readers say things that bear upon our own reading, and upon our responsiveness to our own children as readers and to those we teach. They make us more alert to possibilities and opportunities in talking to children about books, and in working with them: what we actually decide to do is for us to devise, and cannot be had upon prescription. (Fry, 1985, p. 5)

In contemporary society, 'the text' is a plural and multiform artefact; it is symbolic and also intangible; it is, above all, a concept:

But words convey nothing except by a previously acquired meaning, which may be somewhat modified by their present use, but will not as a rule have been first discovered on this occasion. In any case, our knowledge of the things denoted by words will have been largely acquired by experience, in the same way as animals come to know things, while the words will have acquired their meaning by previously designating such experience, either when uttered by others in our presence or when used by ourselves. Therefore, when I receive information by reading a letter and when I ponder the message of the letter, I am subsidiarily aware not only of its text, but also of all the past occasions by which I have come to understand the words of the text, and the whole range of this subsidiary awareness is presented focally in terms of the message. The message or meaning, on which attention is now focussed, is not something tangible: it is the conception evoked by the text. (Polanyi, 1969, p. 92)

Our conception of the literacies of the future will require new strategies in schools; strategies based only on the ability to make meaning from print will no longer do. We already live and work in multiliterate communities; it is very clear that the pace of accelerated communications change will continue to increase. If the process of schooling in such fast-changing conditions is to continue to touch both the hearts and the minds of young people, new approaches to literacy are essential. This, as I have already said, will require new types of training for tomorrow's teachers. It will also of course require that substantial curricular alterations be made to the schooling process in Western society, in a short timeframe, with consequent changes to the courses and methods to be followed and used in schools. All this is achievable, provided only that the state school system is planned, managed and resourced in order to achieve and maximize the huge potential benefits a truly multiliterate society will have, both for the state and for the imaginative and creative potential of all its future people.

References

FRY, D. (1985) *Children Talk about Books: Seeing Themselves as Readers*, Milton Keynes, Open University Press.

POLANYI, M. (1969) *Personal Knowledge: Towards a Post-Critical Philosophy*, London, Routledge and Kegan Paul.

SARLAND, C. (1991) *Young People Reading: Culture and Response*, Milton Keynes, Open University Press.

WILLIAMS, R. (1958) *Culture and Society*, Harmondsworth, Penguin Books.

Notes on Contributors

Neil Campbell is Head of American Studies in the Division of Humanities at the University of Derby, England. He previously trained as a secondary school teacher and worked in a sixth-form college in Leicestershire. His current research interests are in youth culture and African-American literature, areas on which he has also published. He also contributed to *Towards 2000* (Falmer Press, 1995) and is presently co-writing a book on American cultural studies, *Approaching America*, to be published by Routledge in 1996.

Bjørg B. Gundem is Professor of Education at the Institute for Educational Research at the University of Oslo, Norway. Her current research interests and teaching are in didactics and curriculum studies in an international/comparative context. She has published widely in Scandinavia and internationally. Recent publications include *Skolens oppgave og innhold: En studiebok i didaktikk* (The Aims and Content of Schooling: A Course Book in Didactics), (1991) (3rd ed.), Universitetsforlaget, and *Mot en ny skolevirkelighet: Laereplanenei i et sentraliserings-desentraliseringsperspektiv* (Towards a New Reality of Schooling: Curriculum and the Local-National Dilemma), (1993), Oslo, Ad Notam Gyldendal.

Tanja Janssen is Educational Researcher at the Kohnstamm Centre of Educational Research (SCO-Kohnstamm Instituut) and at the Graduate School of Teaching and Learning (ILO) of the University of Amsterdam, Netherlands. Her research interests include the teaching of written composition and literature in secondary education. She has published widely, sometimes with Gert Rijlaarsdam, on literacy issues in the Netherlands and also on a wider international front, especially on issues connected with the teaching of literature.

Ed Marum is Head of the Division of Humanities in the School of European and International Studies at the University of Derby, England. He is also the programme leader in children's literature. He has taught in a variety of schools and has also been English Adviser for Liverpool and a General Inspector in London. He recently edited *Towards 2000: The Future of Childhood, Literacy and Schooling* (Falmer Press, 1995). Currently, he is writing another Falmer Press book, *Contexts for Literacies: Reading, Personal Values and School Experience*, to be published in 1997.

Gert Rijlaarsdam is Associate Professor of Education at the Graduate School of Teaching and Learning (ILO) of the University of Amsterdam, Netherlands.

His PhD was in Social Sciences (Education), on an effective written curriculum. Among his research interests are mother tongue curricula, particularly written composition, writing processes and the large scale assessment of literacy. He has published widely in the Netherlands and internationally, sometimes with Tanja Janssen, on literacy issues.

John S. Simmons is Professor and Coordinator, English Education, Florida State University, USA. He is the author of a considerable body of work on English and reading. Previous responsibilities have included chairing the Conference on English Education (NCTE) and the International Assembly on Teaching English (NCTE). He has been Overseas Visitor to the University of East Anglia. His research interests include critical reading and young people, censorship and language in US schools. His most recent publication is *Censorship: A Threat to Reading, Learning, Thinking,* (1995), International Reading Association.

Index